DATE DUE

DEMCO 38-296

THE SULTANATE
OF OMAN

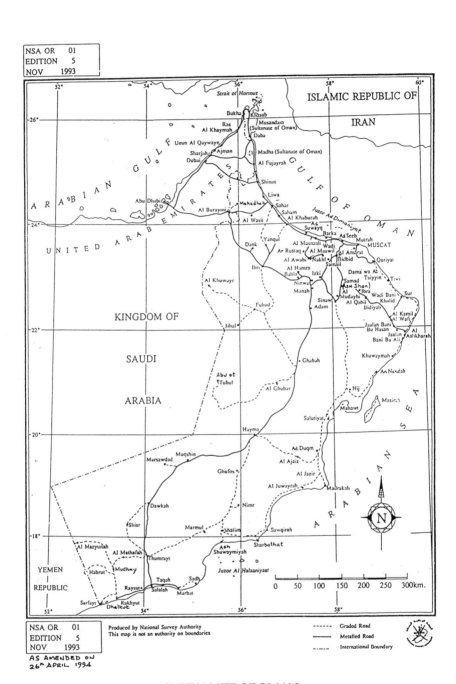

SULTANATE OF OMAN

THE SULTANATE OF OMAN

A Twentieth Century History

MIRIAM JOYCE

 PRAEGER

Westport, Connecticut
London

Library of Congress Cataloging-in-Publication Data

Joyce, Miriam.
    The Sultanate of Oman : a twentieth century history / Miriam
Joyce.
       p.   cm.
    Includes bibliographical references (p.   ) and index.
    ISBN 0–275–95222–3 (alk. paper)
    1. Oman—History.   I. Title.
DS247,068J69   1995
953.53—dc20   95–4268

British Library Cataloguing in Publication Data is available.

Library of Congress Catalog Card Number: 95–4268
ISBN: 0–275–95222–3

First published in 1995

Praeger Publishers, 88 Post Road West, Westport, CT 06881
An imprint of Greenwood Publishing Group, Inc.

Printed in the United States of America

The paper used in this book complies with the
Permanent Paper Standard issued by the National
Information Standards Organization (Z39.48–1984).

10 9 8 7 6 5 4 3 2 1

In memory of David Ben Rafael

CONTENTS

ACKNOWLEDGMENTS

I had considerable support while writing this book. My colleagues at Purdue University Calumet were most helpful and I was assisted by a 1994 Purdue Research Foundation Summer Faculty grant. I owe enormous thanks to Professor Doris Pierce and my present chairman, Professor Saul Lerner.

I am especially grateful to the government of the Sultanate of Oman for providing me with the opportunity to visit the sultanate and interview Omani officials, who were extremely generous with their time. I am indebted to His Excellency, Minister of Information Abdul Aziz Al Rowas for his kindness and unfailing patience. I also appreciate the assistance provided by Lisa Kepinski at the Omani Embassy in Washington. In addition, I am grateful to Professor Norman Itzkowitz for reading an early draft of my manuscript and providing guidance.

As always, I am thankful for the constant encouragement of my honorary daughter Isa Ben Rafael, my Chicago cheering section, Michael and Lisa Wallk, and Stacy and Warren Rubin-Silver. I also want to express appreciation to my children Joshua Haron, Leah Azoulay and Adam Haron. My final thank you is reserved for Salim M. Almahruqi, at the Embassy of Oman,who from the outset of this project was a source of encouragement, information, and equanimity.

INTRODUCTION

Located in the southeastern portion of Arabia, virtually cut off from the rest of the peninsula by the Rub al-Khali desert, the Sultanate of Oman covers an area of 312,000 square kilometers. Oman borders on Saudi Arabia and the United Arab Emirates to the west, Yemen to the south. To the north Oman is bounded by the Strait of Hormuz, to the east the Arabian Sea. The sultanate's coastline extends for 1,700 kilometers and several islands are located near its shores, including Masirah and al Halaaniyaat. Most Omanis are members of the Ibadhi sect of Islam, a sect that emerged in the middle of the eighth century. The Ibadhi followed the Kharijites who believed that the office of head of the community, the imamate, belonged to the most worthy among them. Any Muslim, regardless of his origin, was eligible for the position. Once in office, the imam was required to act impartially, in accordance with the laws of the Shariah. When an imam was considered unjust, he was deposed; if no other candidate was deemed suitable, the office remained vacant. As a result, succession usually brought a crisis, sometimes civil war.

Until the discovery of the Cape of Good Hope and the sea-route to India, Omani Arabs enjoyed a practical monopoly carrying the trade of the East. But then the Portuguese, in 1507, sacked Muscat and took control of the coastal areas of the sultanate. Their chroniclers left warnings about the climate, reporting that the heat was so great swords melted in their scabbards and gazelles roasted in the chase.[1] The Portuguese controlled the coast until 1650, when Omanis, under the leadership of a member of the Yarubi dynasty, Sultan bin Saif, drove them out. After liberating Muscat, the sultan established a wealthy state with possessions in East Africa. Under his successors, Oman continued to prosper. But, as a result of yet another civil war, in 1737, the Persians occupied a portion of the coast. Founder of the Al Bu Said dynasty, Ahmed bin Said, in 1748, liberated Oman. He was elected imam and later sultan, establishing the dynasty. After his death, however, the functions of sultan and imam were completely separated, and the seat of government was moved from Rustaq in the interior to Muscat on the coast.

The most illustrious member of the Al Bu Said dynasty, in the nineteenth century, was Sultan Said (1807-1856). During the first quarter of his reign an Italian observer described the busy port of Muscat:

> The port of Mascat is circular, and is formed by an islet about an Italian mile in circumference, which is immediately opposite the city and renders the anchorage very secure; some wells in the neighborhood afford a supply of excellent water; vegetables, and fruit also abound; the latter consists of dates, lemons, oranges & etc. Poultry are reared in large quantities, the cattle are numerous, and to be bought very cheaply. The sea affords plenty of fish, which, together with rice and dates form the chief sustenance of the inhabitants; and the surplus of oxen, cows, and other cattle. [2]

Sultan Said labored to extend Omani influence. He established a large navy and embarked on numerous sea voyages. His dominions included portions of Arabia, and the Gulf area, as well as considerable territory along the west coast of Africa. Zanzibar, an important trading center in the era before the steamship, became the second capital of his empire. There he installed clove plantations, which together with the slave trade, provided considerable income.

European nations and even the United States established relations with Oman. The British East India Company, in 1798, and the French government, in 1807, concluded treaties with Muscat. At the beginning of the nineteenth century, President

Andrew Jackson sent a special mission to Oman. As a result in September 1833, the Sultanate of Oman and the United States signed a Treaty of Commerce and Navigation -- the first such treaty Washington signed with an Arab state. The president's representative, Edmund Roberts, reported:

> The Sultan of Muscat is a very powerful prince. He possesses a more efficient Naval force than all the native Princes combined from the Cape of Good Hope to Japan. His resources are more than adequate to his wants -- they are derived from Commerce, running himself a great number of merchant vessels -- from duties on foreign merchandise and from tribute money -- and presents received from various Princes. [3]

After the death of Sultan Said, the empire he had established was divided between his two sons; Zanzibar was separated from Muscat. Both Sayyid Majid, the late sultan's oldest son, who was established in Zanzibar, and his younger brother, Thuwayni, governor of Muscat, wanted to succeed their father. The British, now a major power in the Gulf, arbitrated the dispute. Viceroy of India, Lord Canning, proposed that Majid rule Zanzibar and Omani African territories, while Thuwayni rule Muscat and Oman. In order to compensate Oman for the loss of African revenue, Majid agreed to pay his brother MT $40,000 annually. [4]   In 1861, the British intervened to insure payment. Then France recognized the partition of the Omani empire, in 1862, when Paris and London issued a joint declaration pledging to respect the independence of the sultans of Muscat and Zanzibar. The division of Sultan Said's territories was an important factor in the decline of Muscat, which no longer benefitted from the profits formerly derived from slave trading, piracy, and gun running.

Thuwayni continued to rely on the British, who in order to safeguard the imperial lifeline linking Britain to India, had assumed defense of the Gulf and, in 1839, captured the port of Aden, establishing a colony, which became an important naval base and, after the opening of the Suez Canal, a refueling port for ships sailing through the canal, down the Red Sea to India. In the course of the nineteenth century, the British signed protection treaties with many of the sultanate's neighbors. These treaties stipulated that local rulers in the gulf agreed to permit Britain to control their foreign relations, that without first obtaining British permission they would not make treaties or cede territory to any foreign power. In return, the Royal Navy guaranteed their independence and the security of the Gulf. Although Muscat had not signed such an agreement, when Saudi forces, in alliance with the Bani Bu Ali tribe, occupied Omani territory in August 1865, the British supported the sultan and his Omani allies, who assembled to drive the Saudis from the Buraimi Oasis. Soon after the Saudi challenge to the sultan's territory was foiled, internal strife weakened the sultanate. Thuwayni was assassinated by his son Salim, and, in 1868, Salim was deposed by a cousin, who was himself later killed. Meanwhile, British influence increased and, in 1873, Britain assumed responsibility for payment of the Zanzibar subsidy.

At the end of the nineteenth century the Sultanate of Muscat, Oman and Dependencies was a declining state, growing steadily weaker. Tribal warfare was a constant, and the sultan became increasingly more dependent on British support. Prior to the independence of India, in 1947, the senior British representative in Oman held two titles. He was the resident consul and reported to the foreign office; at the same time, he was the political agent, subordinate to the political resident in the Persian Gulf, who reported to the government of India. Yet, despite Britain's strength in the region, the sultanate retained its status as an independent power and never became a British protectorate. During the twentieth century, the sultanate was beset by numerous obstacles. Rulers in Muscat struggled against ultra conservative religious forces, Saudi aggression, Marxist subversion, and economic deprivation. Then in the final quarter of the century, the Al Bu Said dynasty faced new challenges: the availability of oil revenue and the British departure from the Gulf. Among the most complex issues addressed by the government was how to build a modern nation-state and, at the same time, maintain the unique heritage and traditions of the Omani people.

NOTES

1. Ronald Wingate, *Not in the Limelight*, London: Hutchinson, 1959, p. 79.

2. Vincenzo Maurizi, *History of Seyd Said*, London: Oleander, 1984, pp. 19-20.

3. Memorandum, Department of State, 19 February 1938, Franklin D. Roosevelt Library, Hyde Park, New York.

4. The currency used in the sultanate until the middle of the twentieth century was the Austrian Maria Theresa dollar.

1

BEFORE THE GREAT WAR

When Sayyid Faisal bin Turki, the second son of the late sultan and an African concubine succeeded his father, Turki bin Said, as ruler of Muscat, Oman and Dependencies, in 1888, he inherited a heavy burden. The treasury was empty and few sources of revenue were available. Empire was a distant memory; the only remnant of Muscat's overseas possessions was the small territory of Gawadur on the Makran coast. Tribal shaikhs in the interior declined to accept his authority and later threatened his capital. London and the government of India attempted to control his policy. As a result of his dependence on Britain, Sultan Faisal agreed, in 1891, to a British request that he undertake to alienate no portion of his territories without the consent of Her Majesty's government.

Frequently, the sultan was forced to rely on British intervention; at the same time, he wanted to limit Britain's role in Muscat-Oman. Hence, when presented with the opportunity, Sultan Faisal attempted to thwart representatives of the government of India by exploiting his contacts with European powers competing with Britain for influence in the Gulf. In an effort to emphasize the independent status of the sultanate, Sultan Faisal and later his heir, Sayyid Taimour, even encouraged a reluctant Washington to maintain a presence in Muscat.

The sultan governed according to the Koran and Muslim custom. Muscat was ruled personally by the sultan; other towns were administered by his appointed walis (governors).[1] Although the walis were frequently intelligent men, they lacked formal education and were limited in how they approached the problems of their regions. Hence, at the end of the nineteenth century the rhythm of Omani life continued to follow tribal patterns set down centuries earlier. The strongest loyalty was not to the state, but to the tribe. Blood feuds were frequent. Every free man carried a firearm, and even slaves wore the national weapon, the khanjar (dagger).

Sultan Faisal, who kept a lion as a pet, had little education.[2] Unlike most urban Arabs he could neither read nor write. His manners, however, were pleasant and he had diplomatic skills. Except on state occasions, when visiting Europeans he wanted to follow their customs, dispensing with coffee, sherbet, hullwa, (a candy made from sesame) and perfume. He appreciated western inventions, owned a steam yacht, and operated several telephone lines. At the sultan's request, in June 1912, a five-hundred lamp electric lighting plant was installed in the palace, providing the sultan with the first electricity available in Oman. In addition, the sultan allowed the operation of a commercial lighting and power plant. The Indian engineer employed on the project planned to use two 30 kilowatt dynamos capable of supplying current for 6,000 lamps. Given the extreme heat in Muscat and the difficulty of securing punkah pullers, he proposed one set of machines to drive fans.[3]

Muscat's ruler did not maintain any financial records and was in debt to Indian merchants, who charged exorbitant interest. Local gossip maintained that as a result of corruption in the custom's house he often borrowed what was his own money. In 1912 his annual income was approximately $150,000 dollars. He received $28,000 from the British and the remainder from custom receipts. As well as supporting his family of thirty children he supported his brother, sisters-in-law, nieces, and nephews. At the same time, in the hope of maintaining tranquillity in his domains, he continually paid bribes to tribal leaders. As his debts mounted, his creditors pursued him. In order to avoid their persistent demands, Sultan Faisal did not often leave his palace.[4]

In addition to financial problems, Sultan Faisal's most serious difficulty was competition among various tribes. Tribal rivalry often led to warfare that weakened the state and undermined the sultan. From time to time it appeared that the sultan might lose complete control and that the Al Bu Said dynasty depended on Britain for its very survival. In February

1895, Shaikh Abdallah bin Saleh, accompanied by about 400 men, took Muscat and occupied the sultan's palace. Sultan Faisal and his brother fled to the forts -- Fort Jalali and Fort Mirani -- on either side of Muscat harbor. These forts, initially constructed by the Portuguese, provided an excellent haven from which forces loyal to the sultan bombarded the palace. Fighting in the streets of Muscat continued for a month; losses for both sides totaled approximately 150 men. Finally, the British political resident in the gulf sailed to Muscat from his base in Bushire and restored order.

Among those displaced by the fighting was the only American citizen in Muscat, a missionary who belonged to the Arabian Mission of the Dutch Reformed church, the Reverend Peter Zwenner. The Arabian Mission had been organized in 1889 by three theological students at a seminary in New England. Members of the Arabian Mission considered themselves "to be Divinely called upon to engage in pioneer mission work in some Arabic-speaking country."[5] Zwenner had set up a Freed Slave School and a Christian book store in Muscat. Prior to leaving Muscat for Karachi, the American missionary sought refuge with the British consul, whose house was guarded by a detachment of the 21st Bombay Native Infantry. While the American's home was left unattended, it was looted by forces loyal to the sultan. At the same time, rebel tribesmen looted the bazaar Bible shop, together with shops owned by Indian merchants. Meanwhile, the only American official present in Muscat, Vice-Consul Archibald MacKirdy -- a British subject born in Rothesay, Scotland, who had never visited the United States -- left the American Consulate in the care of his Muslim servants and took refuge on a British ship in the harbor.[6]

By the middle of March, Sultan Faisal was once more in control of his capital. However, the rebels had not been militarily defeated. They left Muscat after the sultan paid handsome bribes to their leading shaikhs and a British warship approached the harbor. Before leaving the city, the rebels set fire to the bazaar and plundered all uninhabited houses.[7] Soon after, the sultan took action to improve the defenses of Muscat and Mutrah. He had new twelve-pound guns placed in his forts and hired forty African palace guards who had earlier served his father. He purchased additional munitions and the newest available rifles. At the same time, Sultan Faisal solidified alliances with the southern tribes.[8]

Once order was restored in Muscat, the Rev. Zwenner returned to preach the Gospel. The 1833 Treaty of Amity and

Commerce between Washington and Muscat made no reference to missionaries. Mackirdy asked for instructions from Washington as to whether, against the wishes of local authorities, American missionaries had the right to print and distribute tracts on religious subjects. The sultan was usually generous in his dealings with members of the Arabian Mission. He provided land for their cemetery, homes and gardens. Sometimes, however, the sultan lost patience. When leaving an audience with Sultan Faisal, one missionary overheard the ruler proclaim: "I take refuge with God from a country that has missionaries in it!"[9]

In December 1897, the sultan wrote to the American Consulate in Muscat, complaining about the activities of Rev. Zwenner. The missionary had published a tract in Arabic, which set out to prove the superiority of Christianity. Sultan Faisal considered Zwenner's work to be offensive and demanded that its distribution cease. According to the ruler, "freedom in Religions does not consist in reviling religions." Without waiting for instructions from Washington, Vice-Consul MacKirdy asked Zwenner to acquiesce to the sultan's wishes. The missionary agreed. MacKirdy told Washington that those who disparaged Islam were unpopular in Oman. MacKirdy speculated that Sultan Faisal realized that in the event of an attack on Zwenner Washington would hold him responsible. As a result, he wished to avoid such an attack.[10]

While the sultan could successfully thwart an American missionary working in his territory, he could not oppose Queen Victoria's navy. France at the end of the nineteenth century began to challenge Britain in the Arab Gulf. Members of the French Chamber of Deputies in 1893 complained that England controlled the gulf and suggested sending a French consular agent to open a register of French dependents in the region. In 1894 a French vice-consular agent was accredited to Muscat, and a registry of French dependents was instituted. Here was a boon for slave traders. In order to avoid search and detention by British naval vessels, Arabs engaged in the slave trade registered for French protection and French ships began to visit Omani ports.

Although Sultan Faisal often needed the British, he resented their control and now saw an opportunity to benefit from the expansion of French influence by indicating a degree of independence from London. In 1898, Sultan Faisal declined to fire the customary salute in honor of Queen Victoria's birthday, and shortly thereafter one of the sultan's slaves insulted a group

of visiting British naval officers. Sultan Faisal apologized for
both incidents. But then there occurred a far more serious
breach, a direct threat to Britain's position in the Arab Gulf and
to the security of India. After the French gunboat *Scorpion*
visited the sultanate in 1898, the British learned that the sultan
had granted the French a concession to establish a coaling
station at Bandar Jissah, five miles southeast of Muscat. After
inspecting the site, the political agent, Major C.G.F. Fagan,
concluded that the harbor could be converted into a naval
fortress.[11] The British considered the concession to the French a
violation of the 1891 Omani agreement with Britain regarding
the non-alienation of the sultan's territory.[12] British guns took
aim at the sultan's palace. Sultan Faisal quickly canceled his
concession to the French.[13]

Sultan Faisal continued to be somewhat embittered and
London wanted a reconciliation with the sultan. A new British
agent, Percy Cox, arrived in Muscat in October 1899. He was
"tall and spare, blond and blue-eyed, with an almost Wellington
nose that was none the less commanding for being somewhat out
of line."[14] Cox's first goal was to gain the sultan's confidence.
Together, the ruler and the Briton, in June of 1900 visited the
port of Sur. The sultan had not visited Sur in twelve years. The
residents were happy to receive their ruler and to proclaim their
loyalty. Some ship owners had taken advantage of French
protection but now presented Sultan Faisal with a written
message, which promised that those who had accepted French
flags would relinquish them. Earlier Mackirdy had personally
seen a Sur dhow filled with African slaves. The dhow carried
French papers and flew the French colors. A British cruiser had
intercepted the dhow, brought it into Muscat harbor, and handed
it over to the French consul, "who very properly freed the slaves,
imprisoned the Arab crew, and condemned the dhow to be
broken up." Yet, prior to this incident the French government
had been informed that under the protection of their flag slave
trade was taking place. The French took no action to end the
practice, to protect the "honor of their flag." British capture of
the dhow flying the French flag helped check the slave trade but
did not end the traffic. When visiting Sur, the sultan suggested
to his subjects that there had been some sort of
misunderstanding. Without special written permission and in
accordance with treaties signed between his government and
other governments he did not permit his subjects to accept
foreign protection.[15] The sultan's visit to Sur appeared to be
successful, but loyalty to Sultan Faisal was more superficial than

substantive. Three years later, the sultan was so distressed about
frequent outbursts of rebellion in Sur that in October 1903 he
briefly considered abdication provided the British would agree to
protect his young son, Sayyid Taimour.[16]
        Quarantine regulations also led to an incident involving
the French flag. Despite the best efforts of British authorities,
diseases that had virtually disappeared in Europe broke out in
Oman. Cholera occurred in the autumn of 1899. According to
reports from Muscat, the disease originated in Karachi, where it
became epidemic among Baluchis residing in a village on the
outskirts of the town. The apparent cause of the epidemic was
polluted water. Once pure water was supplied to the village, the
epidemic subsided. Some of the villagers traveled by sea to
Gawadur, a small town on the coast of Baluchistan that was
ruled by the sultan. These travelers brought the disease with
them.   Native vessels succeeded in evading quarantine and
reached Mutrah, three miles west of Muscat. Approximately 135
people died. According to MacKirdy, those who died had not
taken the medicine available at the British hospital.[17] During the
summer of 1900, a new cholera outbreak was reported in several
small villages. Attempting to escape the disease, villagers left
for Muscat. Upon arrival they were put into quarantine and the
disease was contained.[18] At the beginning of the twentieth
century, bubonic plague also occurred.[19] As a result of these
problems, the British assumed responsibility for sanitary
supervision of the ports of Muscat and Mutrah, and the sultan
authorized British officials to provide facilities for quarantines.[20]
        Control of quarantine gave the British the opportunity to
regulate arrivals and departures and to inspect all ships.[21] A
British mail steamer from Bombay in April 1903 arrived in
Muscat. Among the second-class passengers was an Arab
resident from Sur, Abdallah bin Khamis bin Ali, who was
accompanied by five friends traveling in third class. The five
third-class passengers were sent to the quarantine station situated
in a sheltered bay about three miles southeast of Muscat. Bin Ali
was told that all first and second-class passengers were required
to visit the local medical dispensary every morning for the
following six days. Disregarding instructions, the second day
after his arrival in Muscat bin Ali hired a sailboat. Despite the
objections of the medical authorities, he picked up his five
friends at the quarantine station and sailed for Sur. Sultan Faisal
asked the British consul to dispatch a vessel to apprehend the six
men. Cox instructed H.M.S. *Perseus*, then in Muscat harbor, to
arrest them. The sultan sentenced the six to three months in

prison. Owner of a dhow with French papers, bin Ali now claimed French protection. The sultan admitted bin Ali's right to French protection at sea, but refused to accept his right to French protection once he had landed on Omani territory. The French consul came to the defense of bin Ali and demanded his release. The French cruiser *Infernet* arrived in Muscat on 11 May, and the commodore too demanded the release of the six imprisoned Arabs. At this juncture, to avoid the possibility of becoming involved in just such a confrontation, the sultan was visiting the interior of Oman. His brother, Sayyid Mohammed bin Turki, told the French that in the absence of the sultan he was in charge but had no authority to liberate the men. Three days later, the sultan returned to Muscat. A British cruiser was then at the port, and Percy Cox announced that he would support the sultan's decision to keep the men in custody. Negotiations followed; representatives of all three countries -- Britain, France, and Oman -- came to an understanding. They agreed that the sultan might release the men without handing them over to the French authorities, but that he would write to both the British and French consuls in Muscat, informing them of his action. Prior to completing their sentences, bin Ali and his friends were released from prison and permitted to proceed to Sur. Paris and London agreed to refer this dispute to arbitration, and both the French and British warships sailed from Muscat.[22]

During his tenure as Viceroy of India, Lord Curzon, known as a man who "courted rather than feared responsibility," personally responded to earlier visits by Russian and French warships to the gulf. With a fleet of six British men-of-war and two Indian marine vessels, Lord and Lady Curzon reached Muscat in November 1903. The Curzons traveled on the cruiser *Argonaut*, which was at the time the largest ship ever to have visited the Arab Gulf.[23] Curzon had earlier proclaimed that any Briton who permitted another foreign power to infiltrate into the gulf ought to be hanged as a traitor. Before sailing into Muscat, the viceroy received information that the Russians wanted a coaling station in the sultanate, that perhaps the sultan was contemplating accepting a bribe from Moscow. Sultan Faisal greeted Lord and Lady Curzon with great courtesy, referring to Mary Curzon as a pearl. With British guns trained on the sultan, Curzon brushed aside the compliment to Lady Mary. He emphasized that the pearl was the gulf; it was a priceless pearl.[24] Together with a clear and unequivocal warning that Britain alone had primacy in the gulf, His Majesty's Government attempted to soothe the sultan; during the course of the Viceroy's visit, Sultan

Faisal was invested with the Knight Grand Commander, Order of the Indian Empire.[25] Later, as a result of the Anglo-Russian Convention of 1907, the British were no longer concerned about possible Russian competition in the Arab Gulf. Anglo-French conversation had three years earlier resulted in the Anglo-French entente of 1904. Yet, issues relating to Muscat remained unresolved. The International Court of Justice considered the question of whether France had the right to extend its protection to Omani dhow owners. The decision of The Hague Court, announced in August 1905, favored the sultan and pleased both Faisal and the British. The decision limited valid French papers to those issued prior to the Brussels Anti-Slavery Convention of 1892. New papers could only be granted to men who had been French protégés since 1863 when a Franco-Moroccan treaty and Ottoman legislation put limits on the granting of protégé status. The Hague Tribunal also ruled that dhows flying French flags could claim French protection in Omani water, but such rights were not transferable from dhow to dhow or owner to owner; neither did French protection apply on land.[26] At the same time, The Hague Court of Arbitration affirmed the independence of the sultanate.[27] Hence, Sultan Faisal announced that upon landing in the sultanate every Omani subject came under his jurisdiction; therefore, crimes committed at sea under the French flag would be punished by Omani authorities.[28]

Despite the distance in geography and culture that separated the sultanate from Europe and from the United States, Sultan Faisal followed world affairs. After news reached him of the assassination of President McKinley, he called at the American Consulate on 19 September 1901 to express his aversion to the crime and his sympathy to the United States and to President McKinley's widow. Together with the British and French consuls in Muscat the sultan flew his flags at half mast or three days.[29] In 1902, the first American warship to enter Muscat harbor since the accession of Sultan Faisal, the U.S.S. *Isla de Luzon,* visited the sultanate en route to Aden. The captain saluted the port with 21 guns. Accompanied by the American consul, the captain and officers visited the sultan, who later returned the visit and asked Consul Mackirdy to tell Washington that he would like regular visits from American warships.[30]

Vice Consul Mackirdy wanted Washington to take every opportunity to show an interest in the sultanate. He reported to the State Department in 1905 that the sultan had celebrated the wedding of his eldest son and heir apparent, Sayyid Taimour;

MacKirdy recommended that Washington present the newly-weds with a appropriate wedding gift, perhaps a silver ice water pitcher of American design and workmanship. The political resident had already been authorized by the government of India to present the prince with a silver tea and coffee set valued at $175. The French consul had also been authorized to present a suitable gift. There was precedent for such American gift giving. Sultan Faisal had received a gift from Washington in 1881.[31] The State Department, always reluctant to spend money, agreed to present a gift.[32]

On behalf of the State Department, Consul General at Large for Middle East and African Affairs, Alfred L.M. Gottschalk, in January 1910, inspected the American Consulate, which had opened in 1880. His report illustrated both what was required of Foreign Service officials and Washington's indifference to Omani affairs. The consulate's budget was small; however, one of the questions on the form that Gottschalk had to complete asked if a reduction in budget would interfere with the running of the facility.[33] The State Department had long been interested in reducing expenses in the sultanate and in 1886 had complained that American representatives in Muscat spent too much money celebrating the Fourth of July. The consul defended his entertainment expenses, maintaining that the sultan enjoyed the American diplomatic presence. Throughout the year, Sultan Faisal showed his special regard for the United States. Every evening at sunset when all flags were lowered, the sultan's band played the American national anthem immediately after his own anthem. On American Independence Day, the sultan fired a salute, kept the American flag flying on his principal fort, and visited the American Consulate with a considerable retinue. Refreshments, including, sherbet, lime juice, hullwa, dates, and betel nuts were provided by the consul. The American representative in Muscat told Washington that the expense was necessary and served to maintain good feelings between the two countries. The consul emphasized, "Nothing can exceed His Majesty's courtesy to me as your Representative and his great friendship for the American people."[34]

Gottschalk complained in 1910 that the parsimonious conduct of the post was detrimental to American prestige. The British in Muscat were lavishly equipped; so were the French and the Italians. As was the custom in Muscat, the European consulates had signal flags for decoration and distinctive boats with uniformed rowers. The American Consulate had no decorative flag, and when a boat was needed, American Consul

John Ray used a native canoe paddled by tattered Arabs. Visitors who entered the American consulate were received in shabby surroundings. Guests were at risk for the wooden chairs in the consul's office were so dried out by the intense heat and so brittle that they broke unexpectedly. Muscat was Consul Ray's first diplomatic position. Gottschalk stated that, like all beginners, the young consul took it for granted that European nations would have excellent facilities, while the United States did not. Inspector Gottschalk praised Ray as a conscientious official who conducted his office intelligently. Although Ray, a country boy from Texas without social experience or prestigious family connections, had poor table manners and did not dress properly, he was intelligent. He worked hard, studying Arabic, local conditions, and customs. Gottschalk was confident that Ray would shape up and gain social polish, which, of course, would have to wait for a later posting, since Muscat offered no suitable social opportunity. Gottschalk told Washington that Ray appeared to have no bad habits. He lived economically; his only indulgence was the purchase of books.

Gottschalk pointed out that the United States neglected the Middle East, while European foreign services trained specialists in the Arab world. Given Ray's intellect and language skill, Gottschalk advised Washington to provide him with the opportunity to become such an expert. Muscat, an excellent training ground for Arabic students, and one of the few places in the Middle East where a man could live on $2,000 a year, needed an effective American presence, a consulate of the lowest grade, but one that inspired respect. The sultan of Muscat personally called on all of the consuls accredited to his territory. Clearly, Consul Ray needed new furniture. The consul general suggested a sum be allocated for six to eight chairs, which might be obtained from Bombay or Karachi for $2.50 each. Since the floor matting was only partially covered with rugs, Gottschalk also proposed that Washington add an additional fifteen to twenty dollars. There was also the question of lamps. Although earlier there had been a possibility of its installation, as yet there was no electricity available. Ray had two kerosene lamps, which were his personal property. They did not provide sufficient light. Since Muscat offered no evening diversions or social life, the young consul spent many evenings working in his dim office without a good desk lamp. Good lamps were extremely costly, at least ten dollars.

Unlike the dilapidated American establishment, the British, French, and Italians had well-furnished quarters. The British even had their own post office and a number of Indian army guards. Gottschalk complained that in contrast to the Europeans the Americans looked provincial and cheap, a source of bad jokes and ugly gossip. He emphasized that Oman was firmly in the British sphere of influence, and uneducated traders in Muscat sometimes appeared to be hostile to Americans. Gottschalk wanted to remove the opportunity for jokes at the expense of the United States. He speculated that how Consul Ray addressed the sultan might be a reason for humor. Ray called the sultan, "Your Majesty," while all the other consuls addressed him as "Your Highness." The consul general admitted that the issue was minor, but he insisted that it was the small things that hurt American prestige and marked Americans as provincial.

Gottschalk was upset at the low salaries paid the consulate's local employees. The cost of living in the gulf had increased, but the members of the staff received the equivalent of $4.87 monthly. Their salaries was much lower than the salaries paid by the European consulates and was an incentive for dishonesty. Gottschalk recommended an immediate increase for each local employee as well as a uniform consisting of a long blue robe, girdle, and turban, as was the custom in Muscat. In addition, Gottschalk wanted each man to be supplied with a silver dagger. True, daggers were expensive, approximately twenty dollars each, but the daggers would merely be on loan and would remain consulate property.

A major source of pressure to retain the consulate was the Arabian Mission of New York, which had headquarters in Muscat. Commerce with the United States, restricted to the export of dates, was not a factor. There were only three shippers in Muscat who sent goods to the United States, and they generated approximately twenty yearly invoices. Obstacles to increasing trade appeared to be insurmountable. No banking facilities existed in the sultanate, and communication with the United States was slow and expensive. In addition, the vast majority of the sultan's subjects were Bedouin; hence there was a shortage of consumers for goods other than cotton material and arms. Gottschalk suggested that it might be possible to sell cheap American rifles. But American guns in Oman could very well result in objections from the British, who assumed the right to police the Arab Gulf.

During his stay in Muscat, the sultan graciously received Gottschalk. The consul general was pleased. However, when he sailed from Muscat harbor, no guns were fired in salute. Here was yet another indication of lack of respect for the United States. Agitated, Gottschalk complained to the State Department that he believed officers of his rank in most foreign services would have insisted on a salute.[35]

The American consul visiting Oman had the luxury of worrying about prestige, while the ruler of the sultanate had to concentrate on maintaining control as he moved from crisis to crisis. Violence continued to plague the country; friction among the tribes and dissatisfaction with various walis was ongoing. When peace was restored in one area, conflict erupted in another. Tribes in Sohar, in the spring of 1910, accused their walis of oppression and took up arms. Sultan Faisal traveled to Sohar to restore order. He promised to investigate charges against the walis and distributed "a few well-placed bribes." Meanwhile, it appeared there would be more trouble in Sur, where tribal leaders were dissatisfied with the size of bribes they had received to keep the peace.[36] Episodes of violence continued. Fighting broke out in May 1911 between the residents of two villages near Khaburah in Batinah. Approximately twenty people were killed and 150 injured. All the houses in the defeated village were burned to the ground. The immediate cause of the violence was a quarrel between two men, one from each village. Both claimed a dead jujube tree worth ten cents. The minister of war was sent to restore order. At the same time, Isa bin Salih, son of one of the leaders of the band that captured Muscat in 1895, attacked a fort near Sur. Shaikh Isa was considered the amir of Sharkiyah and had a large following among the Hinawi faction. The sultan sent his yacht to Sur and bin Salih was driven back into Sharkiyah.[37] Unfortunately, tension heightened again with the assassination in March 1912 of the Shaikh of Rustaq, a rival claimant to the imamate and an enemy of the sultan. Now Muscatis were concerned that the men of Rustaq would blame the sultan for the shaikh's murder, and perhaps launch an attack against the city similar to the attack that had been mounted in 1895. Additional guards were posted at the gates of Muscat. There was also anxiety that as a result of the tense situation the men of Muscat and Mutrah would be prevented from picking the dates that were ready for harvest in the interior.[38]

Concerned with the constant violence in Muscat, the British guardians of the Arab Gulf wanted to reduce the availability of arms in the sultanate. The government of India had long pressed for an end to arms traffic. The sultan had agreed in 1891 to restrict the flow of weapons into his Gawadur territory, but Sultan Faisal relied on the revenue he received from the customs duty on arms and, hence, declined to interfere with the flow of weapons into Oman.[39] In 1898, pressed by the British, Faisal issued a proclamation permitting British and Persian ships to search vessels flying Omani flags in Omani, Persian, and Indian waters. The British were permitted to confiscate any arms. However, under the French flag the arms trade continued.[40]

Sir Percy Cox, now political resident in Bushire, in the fall of 1911, personally attempted to obtain the Omani ruler's agreement to end all arms traffic. He failed to reach an agreement and returned to Muscat in February 1912 to continue discussions. Cox suggested that all imported arms be placed in a bonded warehouse under the careful supervision of a seconded British officer.[41] To encourage the sultan, who was perpetually plagued with financial problems, in return for a decree ending arms traffic London offered a large annual pension.[42] Although pleased with the pension proposal, Sultan Faisal rejected the idea of supervision by a British officer. Finally, agreeing to appoint a retired Arab employee of the Uganda post office as supervisor of the proposed arms warehouse, the sultan in June 1912 issued the regulations sought by the British:

> Whereas large quantities of arms and ammunition are at present stored without proper control in private buildings distributed in this our town of Muscat, and thus exposed to the risks of attack, robbery or fire, we, impressed by the serious menace to the safety of our capital arising therefrom, have resolved to remedy this state of affairs.[43]

In June 1912, the sultan informed the American consul in Muscat, Homer Brett, that starting the following September all arms and ammunition in his territory were to be stored in a special storage facility. Explaining the reasons for this new regulation, Sultan Faisal said that as a result of the absence of arms control the capital was not safe. The sultan ordered that all weapons imported into his territory be taken directly from the ships that carried them to the special arms warehouse. He also ordered all arms dealers to deposit any stock already on hand in this warehouse and warned that the stock of any trader who did not comply would be confiscated. Special licenses personally signed by the sultan would be issued for the withdrawal of arms, and all arms leaving the warehouse would be marked with a serial number.[44] According to Consul Brett, the sultan had not truly wanted to issue the new regulations but was pressured to do so by British India. The superintendent of the arms warehouse was a British subject who consulted the British consul prior to releasing arms. Arabs who were able to obtain permits rejected them, considering the stamped rifles an indication of subjugation to the British, an insult to their honor. The new regulations infringed on the treaty rights of various powers, who had been guaranteed freedom to trade with Muscat. Americans, however, were not affected because no American citizens were engaged in the arms trade, nor were American arms imported into the sultanate. French merchants, however, were active in the trade and Paris protested, warning the sultan that he was responsible for any loss to French merchants. In Muscat the French consul refused to require his nationals to obey the regulations.[45]

New arms regulations did not end the traffic in weapons. The French continued to trade, carrying arms in small boats flying the French flag "and -- in bravado -- they have the boxes opened and pass as closely as possible to the British flag-ships so that the nature of their cargo can be plainly seen."[46] Consul Brett suggested that the suppression of the arms trade was more important to Britain than the continuation of that trade was to France; he predicted that some sort of compromise between the two European powers would soon be arranged, permitting compensation to French merchants. Britain could not afford to lose prestige. It appeared that despite the 1862 Anglo-French agreement to respect the independence of Oman, at the first indication that any power intended to coerce the sultan, London would declare Muscat British territory.[47] A British squadron composed of six ships commanded by the commander-in-chief of the British naval forces on the East Indies station, Rear Admiral Sir Alexander Bethell, sailed into Muscat harbor on 30 September 1912 and remained until 2 December. Consul Brett suggested that the departure of the British squadron probably indicated an Anglo-French agreement concerning arms traffic. But French traders continued to do business with stocks on hand with no indication that their supply was near exhaustion.[48] Paris and London finally arrived at an agreement. The British took over the stocks of the French arms traders operating in Muscat. After an inventory was completed, the French warehouses were closed under the seals of both the French and the British consuls. [49]

Suppression of arms traffic angered the tribes of the interior. Rebels claimed that the sultan sold his country in return for a personal pension. They issued a manifesto charging Sultan Faisal with failure to enforce Islamic law. They accused him of tolerating alcohol, tobacco, and prostitution in his domains. He was criticized for allowing the beating of drums and the wearing of long mustaches and short beards. They claimed that the sultan did not punish immorality or dishonesty. One indication of the seriousness of the revolt was that it began at the beginning of the date harvest, throughout Arabia usually a period of "profound peace." In order to stem the revolt, the cash poor sultan pressed the British consul for a loan and dispatched his adult sons to various tribes in an effort to detach members from the coalition set up against him. All roads out of Muscat were closed; no produce entered the city. The stallkeepers in the Mutrah bazaar packed their possessions and took refuge on vessels in the harbor. Consul Brett speculated that the British would not permit either Muscat or Mutrah to fall and if necessary would land British troops. [50]

Some shaikhs wrote to the sultan calling him a traitor and threatening to murder any foreigners who approached their spheres of influence. Two groups, hereditary enemies, Hinawi and Ghafri, discarded their traditional animosity and agreed on the election of an imam. The leader of the revolt was the blind mullah Salim bin Hamid, who was believed able to perform miracles. His son-in-law, Salim bin Rashid, who was reported to have inherited his father-in-law's ability to perform miracles was elected imam. The sultan had no force available to meet the threat of a united Hinawi-Ghafri resistance. [51] Insurrection flared in the summer of 1913; in the interior, one town after the other fell to the rebels. Finally, Sultan Faisal dispatched a force of 3,000 men. Almost all of the sultan's troops deserted to the enemy with their arms, ammunition, and supplies. At the end of June 1913, the most powerful shaikh in the country, Isa bin Saleh, joined the rebels. Continuing from victory to victory on 5 July, the rebels occupied the date-producing Samail Valley. The sultan's second son, Sayyid Nadir, with sixty followers, was for a time under siege in Samail. The sultan issued orders that all those who lived outside the walls of Mutrah and Muscat -- more than half the population -- pack up their valuables and move inside the city walls. As a result, the town was crowded with undisciplined tribesmen who were fully armed. "These semi-savage defenders within cause the inhabitants as much fear as does the threatened attack."[52]

Within Muscat itself there were indications that not all residents supported the sultan. It appeared that even the sultan's brother favored the rebels. Unable to control the situation, the unhappy Sultan Faisal appealed to the British. Three British cruisers steamed into the harbor. Visiting the American Consulate on 4 July, the distressed sultan remarked that the rebels might become responsible for what they most feared, British occupation. According to the sultan, after having been defended in his own capital by British troops, his few remaining shreds of independence would have vanished. Meanwhile, the French consul issued arms and ammunition to his dependents. Contrary to the situation inside all other consulates in Muscat, the American consul had no arms to distribute. He reported to Washington that in the event of real necessity he would borrow weapons.[53]

Two hundred fifty British soldiers landed in Mutrah on 9 July and were quartered in a castle two miles outside the town. The situation remained critical.[54] The rebels continued to achieve one success after another, capturing the towns of Bid-bid, Samail, and Nakhal. The sultan's son, Sayyid Nadir, however, was allowed to leave Samail. Meanwhile, the sultan sent three expeditions to the interior. All three groups return to Muscat, demanding more money.[55]

The rebellion appeared to affect the sultan's health. According to palace sources, the ruler had difficulty sleeping, chain-smoked cigarettes, and sometimes appeared to be mentally ill. Prior to the conclusion of the rebellion in October 1913, the unfortunate Sultan Faisal died. His son, Sayyid Taimour bin Faisal, became sultan during a difficult period. The new sultan had been raised with an understanding of the importance of his British connection. Accompanied by Sir Percy Cox in 1903, Taimur bin Faisal had visited Delhi to attend the Great Coronation Durbar of Edward VII. On that occasion the young prince had presented a gold-scabbard sword to the viceroy and had received a machine gun and a cannon for his father's steamer.[56] Ten years later, at the beginning of his reign, the sultan knew that he could count on the British but was uncertain about the loyalty of his own people or the stability of his country. The new sultan attempted to inspire confidence in his leadership. Hoping to mend the rift with the tribes of the interior. Sultan Taimour prohibited smoking, and the use of alcohol. These measures, however, did not satisfy the rebellious tribes. From the middle of March 1914, rebel activity increased. The British intervened to support the new ruler and dispatched ships to shell rebel troops.[57]

The imam, Salim bin Rashid, then wrote a letter to the American government, protesting British interference in Omani affairs. Washington instructed Vice-Consul Mohammed Fazel, a British subject who had replaced Mackirdy, not to respond.[58] In addition to addressing complaints to Washington, shaikhs loyal to the imam directly confronted British officials. The British had ignored the teachings of Islam; they had permitted what was forbidden, the sale of wine and tobacco, and had prohibited what was sanctioned, trade in arms and slaves.[59]

In the months after the outbreak of the Great War, German propaganda reached Oman and strengthened the resolve of the rebels who understood that the British had considerable problems elsewhere. After Turkey joined the central powers in October 1914, rumors circulated that Kaiser William had converted to Islam. He was now Haji Mohammed Guillaume and in his war against the Christians his military was proceeding from victory to victory.[60]

At the beginning of 1915, Shaikh Isa bin Salih and the imam led 3,000 men in an effort to overthrow Sultan Taimour. Shaikh Isa's men were no match for the British. A British-Indian garrison of 700 troops achieved a decisive victory at Bait-al-Falej. Three hundred fifty Arabs were killed and 150 wounded. Reporting to Washington about the rebel defeat, Deputy Consul Fazel wrote, "The Arabs had a good lesson this time. I do not think they will dare to make any more mischief in the near future."[61] The viceroy visited Muscat in February, and offering the services of the British agent as mediator, suggested that the sultan attempt to arrange a settlement. Sultan Taimour invited the rebels to enter into negotiations. His invitation was interpreted to be a sign of weakness, an indication that the central powers were winning the war. Hence, the imam continued to call for a Jihad (holy war). Thus, as the Great War progressed, the breach between the sultan and the tribes in the interior of Oman continued, fueled partially by deep-seated animosities transmitted from generation to generation and partially by the impact of modern European politics.[62]

A year after the death of his father, Sultan Taimour bin Faisal ordered the guns at Fort Mirani to fire a twenty-one gun salute to mark the end of the required period of mourning. Foreign consuls in Muscat then paid official visits to the palace. The sultan told the American representative that he had photographs of presidents Roosevelt and Taft and asked Deputy Consul Fazel for a photograph of President Wilson.[63] Soon after Washington decided to close the Muscat consulate. At this juncture the United States had only one representative in Muscat, Mohammed Fazal. Born in Bombay, a Khoja Indian with British nationality, Fazal like his predecessor, Archibald MacKirdy, had been employed by the Jack Towell Company, which acted as agents for the British India Line, Lloyds, and the Standard Oil Company. The company also exported pomegranates and dates to India and the United States. Fazal purchased W.J. Towell in 1906. He paid 11,000 rupees, approximately $3,400. Business flourished and the American representative bought the small oasis village of Ayyint as a summer residence for his family.[64]

Vice-Consul Fazal had little to do in his capacity as the American representative in Muscat beyond looking after the interests of a few American missionaries and certifying several yearly invoices of dates shipped to the United States; Fazal received instructions to cease operations in March 1915. He was ordered to ship the consulate archives and furniture to Baghdad. Employees of the British Consulate assisted Fazal to close the consulate. They helped remove the flag staff in front of the consulate building. As a result, a rumor spread through Muscat that the American Consulate had closed because the United States joined Germany and declared war on Great Britain. Angry British residents in Muscat had, therefore, pulled down the American flag and broken the flag pole. Meeting with the sultan, the British consul called the rumors "absurd." Perplexed, the sultan asked why Washington had so suddenly decided to close the consulate. The British representative explained that the closure was simply a matter of reorganization.[65] Sultan Taimour asked Fazal to tell Washington that he regretted the American decision to close the American consulate and hoped the United States would reconsider and agree to maintain a presence in Muscat. The State Department assured Sultan Taimour that Washington had only the most friendly feelings toward the sultanate and that on some future date the consulate would, indeed, reopen.[66] Meanwhile, British Foreign Secretary Sir Edward Grey instructed his consul in Muscat that in the absence of a United States official he was authorized to use his good offices for the protection of American interests.[67]

During the course of the Great War the sultanate, remained crucial to the British, and after the defeat of the central powers the Arab Gulf became a truly British lake. Sultan Taimour had no illusions about British power. Unlike his father,

Faisal bin Turki, he had no possibility of even courting a French or a Russian alternative, and the United States had clearly opted out. The sultan was powerless to adopt any sort of independent policy. At the same time, he knew that the tribes in the interior were fiercely independent. Sultan Taimour recognized that the British agenda included support for the Al Bu Said dynasty, and that without foreign assistance he was unable to control his own country. The sultan had no choice but to acquiesce to the marriage of convenience between Muscat and the government of India.

NOTES

1. Report, Brett, Muscat, 2 April 1912, RG 890.00/7, National Archives (hereafter cited as NA).

2. Wendell Phillips, *Oman: A History,* London: Reynal, 1967, p. 149.

3. Memorandum, Brett, Muscat, 25 June 1912, RG 890.00, NA.

4. Report, Brett to Secretary of State, Muscat, 2 April 1912, RG 59 890a 00/7, pp. 2-3, NA.

5. Samuel Zwemer and James Catine, *The Golden Milestone,* New York: Revell, 1940, p. 151.

6. Letter, MacKirdy to Strobel, Muscat, 5 March 1895, Dispatch 167, RG 59, NA.

7. Ibid., 13 March 1895, Muscat, Dispatch 168, RG 59, NA.

8. Robert Landen, *Oman Since 1856*, Princeton: Princeton University, 1967, p. 337.

9. Zwemer & Catine, p. 105.

10. Letter, Mackirdy to Day, Muscat, 22 December 1897, Dispatch 178, NA.

11. Ravinder Kumar, *India and the Persian Gulf Region,* Bombay: Asia Publishing, 1965, p. 82.

12. Sir Harold Wilson, *The Persian Gulf,* London: Allen & Unwin, 1959, pp. 238-240.

13. Landen, p. 382.

14. Quoted in Briton C. Busch, *Britain and the Persian Gulf, 1894-1914*, Berkeley: University of California, 1967, p. 157.

15. Ibid., pp. 159-160.

16. Ibid., pp. 178-179.

17. Letter, MacKirdy to Third Assistant Secretary of State, Muscat, 11 October 1899, Dispatch, 182, NA.

18. Letter, Fazal to third Secretary of State, Muscat, 12 July 1900, Dispatch 192, NA.

19. Ibid., 30 January 1900, Dispatch 183, NA.
20. Sir Harold Wilson, *The Persian Gulf,* London: Allen & Unwin, 1959, p. 243.
21. Busch, pp. 173-183.
22. Letter, Mackirdy to Garrett, Muscat, 3 February 1905, Dispatch 197, NA. Also see Busch, pp. 173-179.
23. Muhammad Abdullah, *The United Arab Emirates,* London: Croom Helm, 1978, p. 27.
24. Leonard Mosley, *Curzon: The End of An Epoch,* London: Longmans, 1960, pp. 82-83.
25. Busch, p. 179.
26. Ibid., pp. 183-184.
27. Herbert J. Liebesny, "International Relations of Arabia: The Dependent Areas," in *The Middle East Journal,* Vol. 1, No. 3 , 1947, p. 163.
28. Wilson, pp. 242-243.
29. Mackirdy to State Department, Muscat, 20 September 1901, Dispatch 187, NA. Mackirdy also noted that the British vessel *Sphinx* in Muscat harbor displayed an American flag at half mast in addition to its own flag.
30. Ibid., 9 November 1902, Dispatch 190, NA.
31. Letter, Mackirdy to Assistant Secretary of State, Muscat, 23 January 1905, Dispatch 196, NA.
32. Letter, Fazel to Assistant Secretary of State, Muscat, 12 June 1905, Dispatch 199, NA.
33. Inspection Report, Gottschalk, Muscat, 19-25 January 1910, NA.
34. Letter, Consul to Porter, Muscat, 10 September 1886, NA.
35. Inspection Report, Gottschalk, Muscat, 19-25, January 1910, NA.
36. Letter, Ray to Straus, Muscat, 31 May 1910, RG 59 890a 00/1, NA.
37. Ibid., 28 May 1911, RG 59 890a 00/15, NA.
38. Letter, Brett to Secretaty of State, Muscat, 18 March 1912, RG 59 890a 00/7, NA.
39. Busch, pp. 271-272.
40. Ibid., pp. 273-274.
41. Busch, p. 292.
42. Letter, Brett to Secretary of State, Muscat, 17 February 1912, RG 59 890a 113/14, NA.
43. Quoted in Busch, p. 295.
44. Letter, Sultan to Brett, Muscat, 4 June 1912, RG 59 890a 00/7, NA.

45. Letter, Brett to Secretaty of State, Muscat, RG 59 890a 113/25, NA.

46. Ibid., 18 March 1912, RG 59 890a 00/7, NA.

47. Ibid., RG 59 890a 113/25, NA.

48. Ibid., 2 December 1912, RG 59 890a 00/12, NA.

49. Ibid., RG 59 890a 113/27, NA.

50. Ibid., 2 June 1913, RG 59 890a 00/13, NA.

51. Ibid., 2 December 1912, RG 59 890a 00/12, NA.

52. Ibid., 7 July 1913, RG 59 890a 00/14, NA.

53. Ibid.

54. Letter, Brett to Secretary of State, Muscat, 15 July 1913, RG 59 890a 00/15, NA.

55. Ibid., 11 August 1913, RG 59 890a 00/15, NA.

56. Busch, p. 172.

57. Letter, Fazel to Secretaty of State, Muscat, 7 April 1914, RG 59 890a 00/18, NA.

58. Letter, Secretary of State to Fazel, Washington, 28 May 1914, RG 59 890a 00/20, NA.

59. Gertrude Bell, *The Arab War*, London: The Golden Cockerel Press, 1940, p. 25.

60. Thomas Bertram, "Arab Rule Under The Al Bu Said Dynasty," in *Proceedings of the British Academy*, Vol. 24, No. 1, 1938, p. 48.

61. Letter, Fazel to Secretary of State, Muscat, 18 January 1915, 890.00/23, NA.

62. Bertram Thomas, pp. 49-50.

63. Letter, Fazel to Secretary of State, Muscat, 6 October 1914, 840.7 NA.

64. Michael Field, *The Merchants,* Woodstock, N.Y. Overlook, 1984, pp. 158-160.

65. Letter, Benn to Cox, Muscat, 11 April 1915, R/15/6/147/, India Office Library, London, England (hereafter called IOL).

66. Carr to FazeL, Washington, 17 May 1915, R/15/6/147/, IOL.

67. Telegram 135, Benn to U.S. Duty, Bushire, Muscat, 23 June 1915, R/15/6/147/, IOL.

2

BETWEEN THE GREAT WARS

As a result of the defeat of Turkey and the final collapse of the Ottoman Empire, a victorious Britain emerged from the Great War with additional responsibilities in the Middle East. In July 1922, the Council of the League of Nations approved British acquisition of the mandates for both Palestine and Iraq. But in Muscat-Oman nothing at all had changed. The world war had no impact on the established rhythm of life in the sultanate. Sultan Taimour bin Faisal faced the traditional enemies of his dynasty, rebellious tribes in the interior, and a possible threat from the Saudi ruler, Abdul Aziz bin Saud, whose Wahhabi warriors had seized the Hejaz in 1921 and three years later controlled Islam's holiest city, Mecca. Like his father before him, the sultan had economic problems. Even prior to the worldwide depression that began in 1929, the financial situation of the sultanate was dire. British interests had considered the possibility of finding oil in Oman, but nothing came of early attempts to locate potential drilling sites. Sultan Taimour grew increasingly depressed about conditions in his domains. He did not enjoy his role and as the decade of the twenties progressed was reluctant to perform his duties. The British assumed the responsibility of coaxing the sultan into fulfilling his obligations. When finally he refused, the British supported the continuation of the Al Bu Said dynasty, supervising the transition to the rule of Sayyid Said bin Taimour.

Bertram Thomas, an Englishman who served as financial adviser and later, wazir to Sultan Taimour, traveled throughout the sultanate with the ruler and recorded the customs of the period. Oysters thrived in the salty waters of the gulf, and pearl fishing was an important source of income. During the diving season, from May until October, men moved northward to the pearl banks on the Trucial coast. Fishermen and sailors were lowered into the water by gardeners, and even Bedouin. Holy men also participated. Sometimes exhausted divers came out of the sea complaining of pains, which were attributed to jinns. The holy men cured their afflictions with readings from the Koran.[1] Each diver averaged fifty dives daily, carrying a weight and a bag into which he scooped the oysters. The oysters were collected in a single pile; at the end of the working day they were opened. Most of the pearls found were seed pearls. Divers were paid when the season ended, but a substantial number had to return funds advanced to them at the beginning of the period and did not make a profit. Often divers remained in debt to their captains; these men had to return year after year to work off their debts. Divers' sons inherited their fathers' obligations.[2] This system continued until the decade of the 1930s, when the global depression together with Japanese competition -- the introduction of cultured pearls -- destroyed the market for Arab Gulf pearls.

During the summer months, large numbers of Muscat residents traveled thirty five miles to Sib, which Thomas called the "Brighton of Muscat." Even a poor man with no apparent means of support could take a holiday there. According to custom, he could enter a stranger's date garden. Although removing dates from the trees was considered theft and, of course, forbidden, he could eat dates that had fallen to the ground, sleep in the shade of the trees, and drink from the garden well, remaining as many weeks as he pleased.[3] On journeys throughout his domains, the sultan held the traditional burza (assembly), which took place in the morning, afternoon, and evening. Thomas described such an occasion in the Eastern Batinah. A carpet was put down under a spreading acacia tree. The Bedouin ranged themselves in a large circle. Dates, coffee, and an incense-burner were passed around. According to Thomas, Bedouin were likely to judge a ruler by "the frequency of the coffee cup."[4] The Omani life style that Bertram described appeared in some respects to be similar to life in the sultanate as portrayed by the Italian Vincenzo Maurizi, who had been employed by Sultan Said more than a hundred years before Bertram arrived in Oman. Vincenzo wrote that during the date harvest it was very difficult to engage a servant because the "staff of life" provided everyone with nourishment. Many sat under the trees all day either reciting verses from the Koran or sleeping.[5]

In March 1929, Sultan Taimour bin Faisal took one of his customary inspection trips to view his country and greet his people. He traveled by camel through the Batinah to Sohar, stopping at the headquarters of each province. All of the important shaikhs of the Batinah joined the sultan on his journey, with the exception of the shaikhs of the Yal Saad tribe, excluding Hilal bin Humaid, who unlike the other leaders of his tribe appeared to pay his respects. One of the sultan's goals during this trip was to arrange a peace agreement between two tribes that had clashed, the Hawasinah and the Bani Umar. Sultan Taimour was successful; the two tribes made peace. The sultan also used the journey as an opportunity to move against the continuing trade in slaves. At Sohar, during an open majlis, the sultan arrested a native of Suq al Quabil, Mohammed bin Abdallah al Baluchi, and imprisoned him in the local fort for selling a slave that belonged to his family. The sultan declared to the meeting of tribesmen: "Slavery is no longer profitable and blessed is he that avoideth slaves." During this trip the sultan used a car that belonged to his younger brother, Sayyid Hamid bin Faisal, and traveled a dirt road that Sayyid Hamid had ordered constructed, a road cut through the heart of date groves that covered a path from Saham to Sohar, by way of Liwa Nabar Hasafin, across the salt plain to Shinas and again through palm groves to Abu Baqara. After thirty days on the road the sultan returned to Muscat where he received a twenty-one gun salute fired from Fort Jalali.[6] Concerned that despite the sultan's best efforts the slave trade was continuing in the Batinah, the political resident in Bushire asked Bertram Thomas, in August 1929, to tour the coastal area in a British ship in order to look into the problem. Thomas reported a small but regular slave traffic between the tiny ports of Persian Baluchistan and the Arab coast. British ships in the area carried out searches of passing dhows. News of the searches spread and served as a deterrent but did not end the trade.[7]

Changes did occur, however slowly. As a result of the opening of the Muscat-Mutrah road, by 1930 there were eighteen motor cars in the sultanate. One, a Ford Sedan, belonged to the sultan, who had received it as a gift the year before from American businessman-diplomat Charles Crane. Attracted to the Arab world, Crane had earlier spent twelve days visiting the sultanate.[8] In addition to road construction by the Muscat infantry, prisoners improved the road through the suburbs of Muscat, and at his own expense, the Royal Navy coal contractor,

Khan Bahadur Nasib, began constructing a road from the Wadi
Adai to Qabil. The importance of Muscat as a coaling station for
the Persian Gulf Squadron had increased during the Great War.
So had Nasib's profits. In Sohar the wali began his own road-
building program. The optimistic British political agent in
Muscat predicted that while it was still necessary to convey mail
by the favor of dhow captains, or if the letter was urgent, by
camel courier, it would soon be possible to send letters by car.[9]
He was mistaken. Travel remained difficult.

Meanwhile, in the two decades between the world wars,
missionaries in Oman persisted with "patient plodding." The
sultan and the British often considered American missionaries to
be too independent. Neither the sultan nor the British wanted the
Americans to leave Muscat without permission. It was a matter
of control, but at the same time there was real concern for the
safety of the infidel. En route to take up his post as American
Consul in Baghdad, John Randolph, in 1923, traveled on a
British India Steam Navigation ship that stopped in Muscat for
several hours. Randolph left the ship to call on an American
missionary, Dr. Sarah Hosmon. Dr. Hosman praised the British
authorities. They were helpful and courteous. They had arranged
free customs entry for all supplies sent to the mission. But
Hosman complained that she did not have the right to buy real
estate or to travel when and where she desired.[10] Once in
Baghdad, Randolph continued to receive complaints about
British travel restrictions from medical missionaries in the
sultanate. Even when they were invited by shaikhs in the
interior, guaranteed safe conduct and escorts, the British consul
told the Americans to remain in Muscat. He maintained that the
roads were dangerous, that if anything happened to an American
citizen his government would have to dispatch a punitive
expedition into the interior to punish the guilty "in order to
prevent a loss of prestige by the white man."[11] Finally, however
Dr. Hosman received British permission to travel. Hosman had a
physical disability; she walked with considerable difficulty yet
practiced medicine under the most strenuous conditions. She
briefly visited the interior of Oman in 1924. In the course of a
day in Suwaiq, located in the Batinah Valley -- a twenty six hour
journey from Muscat by sailboat -- she treated the sick from
morning until sunset. Hosman wrote, "I never saw so many bad
eyes in one day's time in all my life." She moved on to Hazm,
where her host was a former governor of Rustaq. She stayed at a
fort, which she called the strongest in Oman, one no Arab could
enter with ordinary guns. She had to walk up several flights of
stairs to reach her room, but the view was worth the difficult

climb. From the windows she could glimpse the sea, miles across the desert.[12]

In 1932, Dr. Harold Storm slipped off to Dhofar without permission. An exasperated political agent wrote to the sultan, "I trust that the American missionaries will realize the folly of their ways and repent their very bad manners."[13] The American Mission in 1937 had five workers, including two physicians. Storm, who had served as a medical missionary in Arabia for eleven years, called the Omanis the most friendly of all the Arabs.[14] Yet, after fifty years of missionary activity, there was no Christian church in Arabia and baptized converts could be counted "on the fingers of both hands." Storm lamented:

> The Moslem heart is a heart of stone, and every appeal of Christianity seems to rebound from it without making much, if any, impression. Yet our friendships, our acts of mercy, kindness and helpfulness in hospitals and schools are received with gratitude. Because of these things the missionary is loved, but not Christ. It is this which causes the missionary to Arabia at times to despair of his task.[15]

Other constants remained: tribal rivalry and conflict between the more cosmopolitan coast and the conservative interior. Nevertheless, in 1920 the sultan and tribal leaders, including the Imam Mohamed bin Abdallah al Khalili, came to an understanding and signed a covenant, the Agreement of Sib. In the autumn of 1920, the sultan was in India, where he had gone to receive his new Turkish bride, so he did not actually attend the signing ceremony. He was represented by the political agent in Muscat, Ronald Wingate. After traveling up the coast from Muscat by dhow, Wingate arrived at the meeting place, a beautiful date garden. Thirty shaikhs met the sultan's representative and his party. For two days they talked and drank cup after cup of coffee. Evenings, after concluding their discussions, they feasted, and later slept on the carpets that covered the ground. On the third day of deliberations a problem arose. The shaikhs insisted that the agreement be concluded between the sultan and the imam. According to Wingate,

> This was fatal, and I knew that I could not possibly agree to it on behalf of the Sultan, for this would mean that the Sultan acknowledged another ruler, and a ruler who was already an

elected spiritual leader and an admitted temporal representative of the tribes.[16]

Hoping to prevent the collapse of negotiations, Wingate told the story of how after the Prophet Mohammed had negotiated an agreement with the people of Mecca at Hadaibiyah, they pointed out to him that the Prophet of God need not sign a peace treaty with mere mortals. As a result, rather than sign Mohammed, Prophet of God, Mohammed signed Mohammed bin Abdallah. Wingate achieved the result he wanted. The assembled shaikhs accepted an agreement between the sultan's government and the representative of the Omani tribes, Isa bin Salih.[17] Later, the British negotiator was rewarded for his service to the sultanate when Sultan Taimour presented him with the two-and-a-half foot high coffee pot with a large curved spout that for many years had perpetually brewed coffee in front of the palace.[18]

The Agreement of Sib permitted local autonomy, but did not recognize Oman as a separate entity, independent from Muscat. nevertheless, the imamate of Oman, headquartered in Nizwa, took every opportunity to express its autonomy. In 1929, followers of the imam passed a resolution saying that in the future the salaries of their chiefs, qadis, and troops would be paid out of funds collected locally. In addition, authorities in Nizwa would purchase new arms and ammunition with these funds. At the same time, the conservative tribesmen requested that the British government prohibit airplanes and motorcars from entering the interior.[19]

The Agreement of Sib did not conclude the sultan's difficulties. Tribal unrest continued. Saudi leader Abdul Aziz bin Saud continued to gain territory and prestige in the postwar period; his Wahhabi followers took every possible opportunity to extend his control and spread their theology. Wearing Arab dress, Captain G.J. Eccles, together with a British convert to Islam, A.F. Williamson, known as al-Hag Abdallah, toured the sultanate as members of the D'Arcy Oil Company's Geological Survey of 1925.[20] Speaking in London at a meeting of the Central Asian Society, in October 1926, Eccles told his audience that without British support the Al Bu Said dynasty would fall.[21] Sir Percy Cox agreed. Although he referred to Ibn Saud as "a very dear friend," the British political resident in the Persian Gulf considered the Saudi monarch to be a potential threat to the sultanate. According to Cox, the Wahhabi ruler planned to regain all the territory his ancestors had controlled a century before and Buraimi, where Sultan Taimour claimed several villages, had earlier been occupied by the Wahhabi. Prior to

World War I, London had paid Ibn Saud a subsidy; in return he agreed not to attack British associates. "Our friends were to be his friends." At the conclusion of the Great War, however, Britain had to cut expenses; Ibn Saud lost his subsidy. The Saudi ruler, now recognized as king of the Hejaz, told Cox that he was entitled to pursue his own policy and work out his own destiny. Cox speculated that Ibn Saud would attempt to take control of the interior of Oman.[22]

It appeared that the Saudi ruler might have an opportunity to expand into Oman when, in October 1928, members of the Bu Ali tribe, who were Wahhabi, led by Said bin Abdallah, occupied a fort at Sur. Attempting to gain support from Ibn Saud, they hoisted a Wahhabi flag. Sultan Taimour had never achieved total control of Sur. He had retained power only by balancing rival tribes. With the hoisting of the Wahhabi flag that symmetry was lost. Unwilling to have Sur fall to the Wahhabi, the imam threatened that if Muscat did not take action, his men would enter the area. The sultan attempted to stop the revolt. He ordered loyalists to fire on the occupied fort. The sultan's men fired twenty five rounds; however, the available gun was too small to do any serious damage. Helpless, the Muscat government asked the British to order the bombardment of the occupied fort. The political resident in the gulf agreed. The government of India opposed the extension of Wahhabi control to Sur and if Said bin Abdallah was not stopped, Britain's prestige would suffer. The British were determined to send a clear message that rebellion would not be tolerated.

If Sur was allowed to slip away from the sultan's territory, Sultan Taimour would lose half of his revenue, and eventually the Saudis would control the interior of Oman. The political resident speculated that bombardment by the British navy would not resolve the problem, that the best and cheapest method was to send an Indian regiment to Sur, selected Indian troops, men who would not be influenced by the Wahhabi movement. The political resident calculated that Indian troops would have to remain in Sur for approximately six months.[23] Since the climate in Sur was mild in the winter, the soldiers stationed there could live in tents.[24] He suggested that the HM *Enterprise*, en route to Karachi, be ordered to Sur.[25]

Whitehall considered the dispatch of an Indian regiment to Sur. The government of India advised that such action was unnecessary. After considering the possibility that Wahhabi forces from Nejd might reach Sur to assist the rebel tribesmen, Delhi concluded that it was unlikely. The route, approximately 400 miles, was a difficult one and some tribes along the route were unfriendly to the Wahhabi. While the British considered what sort of action to take, the situation deteriorated. Additional tribesmen rallied to the cause of Said bin Abdallah. The Bani Riyan, a tribe located on the Jebel Akhdar, together with other Ghafiri tribes of the interior, participated in the movement.[26] The naval commander-in-chief on 5 November offered to send the HM *Effingham* to Sur, but declined to dispatch troops.[27] Refusal to send troops dismayed the political resident, who still feared a possible Saudi movement into Oman. He protested that long marches were not unusual for Bedouin, that just last spring the Ataibah were prepared to march a similar distance to attack Basrah. The political resident in Bushire warned that in the event Ibn Saud's men marched, the tribes on the coast would be incapable of resisting their advance. Sir Lionel Haworth, visiting the Persian Gulf, said he did not wish to be an "alarmist," but he supported the political resident. According to Haworth, the presence of Indian troops would insure that Sur was not lost to the sultan.[28]

The vice-admiral, Commander-in-Chief B. Thesiger arrived in Delhi on 31 October for an official visit with the viceroy. While Thesiger was in Delhi, the situation in Sur continued to deteriorate. At this juncture, there was no regiment immediately available for service in Oman; nor was there transportion. The political resident asked Thesiger if the navy might take some action to resolve the problem without landing troops. Thesiger doubted the navy could permanently resolve the problem, but he agreed to sail to Sur on the HMS *Effingham*, and look over the situation. The viceroy was grateful. Arriving in Sur, Thesiger interviewed the sultan's son, Sayyid Said, who had sailed from Muscat on the HMS *Cyclamen*. Fortunately, the fort controlled by Said bin Abdallah was isolated from the town. It was easy to bombard it without damaging other buildings. The commander-in-chief wished to achieve a psychological as well as a military victory. He declined to fire his own ship's guns in order "to leave the natives to imagine what power we had if we chose to use it." Instead, Thesiger ordered the less powerful HMS *Cyclamen* to destroy the fort because that sloop was always present in the region. After issuing a warning, the HMS *Cyclamen* fired eleven shells, which destroyed the fort, but inflicted no casualties. The Wahhabi flag came down at Sur.[29]

Maintaining British power was, of course, a major concern for London, but at the end of the 1920s it appeared that naval power alone was not sufficient. The British military looked to the development of air power. In the summer of 1929, the British surveyed the Arab Gulf and the Gulf of Oman to locate possible landing grounds suitable for the use of military airports along the air route to India. British officers visited both Trucial Oman and the Sultanate of Oman, traveling overland between the two. For two days the officers were lost in the desert wastes. Returning to their base, they reported that neither Trucial Oman nor the sultanate contained a satisfactory area for a military airport where it would be possible to store emergency supplies. The British, therefore, decided against the immediate establishment of an airport in either location. Instead, London considered the development of flying boats, which in the event of emergency could land in the water. From Baghdad, John Randolph reported to Washington that six such flying boats were already stationed at Basrah. [30]

As the British continued to plan for the maintenance of security in the gulf the sultan grew increasingly discouraged. Sultan Taimour began his reign during a rebellion, and since 1913 his domains had continued to be plagued by conflict and division. The role of sultan was taxing, with too many pressures and too few pleasures. He was frustrated and unhappy. In addition to tribal unrest, he never had enough money to meet his needs. For more than a decade Sultan Taimour discussed his desire to abdicate with British officials. When he first proposed abdication in 1920, the British responded with financial assistance, stipulating that in return the sultan reside in Muscat for at least three months a year. He agreed. The sums provided by London solved some immediate problems for the ruler, but he remained dissatisfied. The sultan enjoyed traveling abroad and grudgingly returned to Muscat only when pressed. Once in Muscat, despite British pressure to assume responsibility, he took only a minor role in the government of his territories.

In 1930, the restless Sultan delegated considerable responsibility to his son, Sayyid Said, and left Muscat, insisting that he would never again return. [31] The newly assigned British consul to Muscat, Major Trenchard Fowle, visited the sultan in Dehra Dun, India in September 1930. Prior to meeting the ruler, Fowle had read reports about how several of his predecessors viewed Sultan Taimour. In 1920 the sultan was called vain, idle, and useless, but nine years later was considered an able man with the potential to rule well. Fowle agreed with the latter depiction of the ruler. He considered the sultan to be intelligent and appreciated his sense of humor. When Fowle visited Sultan Taimour in India, however, the ruler of Muscat was in the midst of preparations for a tiger hunt; yet he maintained that he was in poor health and, hence, unfit to continue as head of state. The British consul was not deterred. He attempted to coax the sultan

into returning to Muscat, listing all the measures the British were
taking to ease the burden of state. His Majesty's government had
worked out a plan to raise custom dues from 5 percent to 7.5
percent and had asked both the United States and France to
agree. At the same time, the political resident had applied to the
government of India for a moratorium on the next repayment of
the State debt. In addition, Lt. Colonel Biscoe had gone to Sur to
induce the Amir of Ja'alan to lower his flag and promise future
cooperation. Finally, Consul Fowle reminded the sultan that his
people needed him, "that what Arabs really appreciated was a
personal ruler." Unable to move Sultan Taimour, the
disappointed British consul asked who he suggested as his
successor. The sultan replied that there were several suitable
candidates, including his son Sayyid Said.

Reporting to Bushire, Fowle suggested that Sayyid Said
would be an able successor to his father but that he was still a
young man, and prior to assuming the responsibilities of sultan
he needed additional preparation. Fowle was not yet prepared to
accept Sayyid Taimour's abdication. He proposed that further
economic pressure might persuade the reluctant ruler to return to
Muscat:

> Personally, as I have already stated, I like the
> Sultan and have no wish to be hard on him, but
> business is business and if he does not choose to
> do his job, I do not see why he should be paid
> for not doing it. The allowance from the State,
> should in my opinion, be the lowest amount
> which will keep him on very ordinary comfort. [32]

After Fowle's visit to Dehra Dun, the political resident in
Bushire, Lt. Colonel Biscoe, reported to the sultan that in order
to raise more revenue for Muscat, he had obtained Washington's
agreement to a proposed increase in the tariff and was still
awaiting French consent. He also reported that yet another tribal
disturbance appeared to be resolved. Shaikh Ali had agreed to
stop flying his own flag at Aiqa. Fowle, however, cautioned the
sultan that the fall in the dollar exchange had adversely affected
the finances of the State and even if additional revenues were
obtained from an increase in the tariff, the government would
have to continue to exercise the most stringent economy. Biscoe
then moved on to the subject of the sultan's proposed abdication,
asking that the sultan meet him in Muscat to discuss the issue. [33]

The sultan once again refused to return to Muscat and
suggested that instead the two meet in Karachi. [34] Exasperated,

Biscoe told Fowle that he would not go to Karachi.[35] Biscoe reported to New Delhi that although the sultan was well enough to go tiger hunting, he continued to use ill health as an excuse to evade his responsibilities. Biscoe maintained that the financial aspect of the sultan's proposed abdication was a serious concern, and, then too, Sayyid Said was only twenty one years old. While in charge of the administration during his father's prolonged absences, he performed well. Perhaps, with British officials to guide him, young Sayyid Said, who had been educated at Mayo College, known as the "Eton of India," would become a good ruler. At present, however, the finances of the state were in dangerous condition. The sultanate could not afford the additional expenses that Sultan Taimour's abdication would necessitate. The political resident advised the government of India to continue applying financial pressure to force the reluctant sultan into returning to Muscat.[36]

Sultan Taimour had considerable personal expenses. He supported the mother of Sayyid Said, his wife in Muscat, a son in Constantinople, an additional wife in Dhofar, who was the mother of two sons and one daughter. Biscoe worked out a strategy to delay the sultan's abdication, suggesting that when the sultan realized that the state "cannot and will not maintain him in comfort and idleness," -- that his income would be greatly reduced -- the sultan might reconsider.[37] At this juncture, the effects of the Great Depression caused yet another decline in Oman's revenue. As a result, the government of India agreed to postpone payment of a loan earlier provided to the sultanate. The contract of a highly paid financial consultant serving in Muscat was not renewed; he was replaced by an official with a lower salary. Lt. Colonel Biscoe continued to express concern that the abdication of the sultan would affect the finances of the state. The sultan's father, Faisal, had received a yearly subsidy from the government of India as compensation for loss of revenue from arms traffic. The subsidy began shortly before the sultan died and at his death had been transferred to his heir, Taimour, but in the event of his abdication the subsidy would cease. In addition, if the sultan abdicated, he would need a pension, which would further increase the burden of the state. The political resident was angry at Sultan Taimour and so was the sultan's son, who told Biscoe, "A private individual proceeding on a journey sets his house in order before he leaves; how much more should the ruler of a state do so!"[38]

Efforts to convince the sultan to return to Muscat continued. In the spring of 1931, Sayyid Said visited his father in India and tried to persuade him to return. The prince failed. While in Karachi, Sayyid Said became ill. He suffered from malaria and an irregular heart beat. Doctors advised that he not immediately return to Muscat and ordered several months complete rest in a hill station.[39] Unlike his father, the prince wanted to return to his responsibilities. Fowle visited Sayyid Said in Karachi and told him to follow doctor's orders, that if he returned to Muscat in the hot weather he would further endanger his health and might in the future always have to spend the hot months outside Muscat, which would clearly not benefit the state.[40]

Sultan Taimour bin Faisal finally prevailed, and in 1932 he abdicated. He was succeeded by his son, Sayyid Said bin Taimour. After the abdication of Sultan Taimour, British intelligence maintained a close watch on both his correspondence and his activities. The government of India was perplexed when in 1935 the former sultan traveled under an assumed name, Alsaid. In Bombay, he booked a second-class ticket for Japan. He traveled with an Iraqi Jew, Moalim Saleh Hayim, who was a naturalized British subject. In Singapore Mr. Alsaid later rented a house and requested that the police not divulge his true identity. While in Singapore the former sultan met with Shaikh Mohammed El Sakoff, an alleged Japanese representative in the kingdom of Saudi Arabia.[41] According to intelligence agents, the former ruler was honest and exercised common sense. He did, however, enjoy night clubs and dancing. At the same time, he took considerable interest in the sultanate and in letters to his son offered sound advice. There was no evidence that Alsaid was engaged in any sort of subversive activity. Intelligence agents also reported that the former sultan planned a second trip to Japan. His motive was neither political nor economic, but romantic. During his previous trip he met a Japanese woman, who fell in love with him.[42]

The new sultan too was concerned about the activities of his family. Sultan Said had a half-brother, Sayyid Tariq bin Taimour bin Faisal, who had been raised by his Turkish mother, Kamile Ilguay, first in Turkey and later in Germany. Tariq's mother stated: "I never for a moment forsook my efforts to bring up my son as a person of use to his country."[43] She permitted Tariq born in 1922 to go to Muscat in 1939. The western educated young prince, a possible candidate to become the future ruler, left behind the cinemas and restaurants of Frankfurt for the strict Muslim society of Muscat. Once in the sultanate, Tariq did not adjust gracefully to walking backward out of his brother's presence. The sultan, meanwhile, was distressed that upon his arrival from Germany his younger brother expressed pro-Nazi ideas. Later, the sultan's concern was allayed; he noted that in Muscat Tariq changed his mind about the virtue of national socialism. In 1939, Sayyid Tariq was sent to Sur to learn about the various tribes from the wali, Saud bin Ali. Later, he became an officer in the Muscat Levies at Bait-al-Falaj, and while serving he asked to go to India for officer's training. Although Tariq wanted military training, the sultan and the British favored police training. Before Tariq's departure for India, in 1942, the political resident in Bushire, Sir Rupert Hay, informed the inspector general of police in Madras that while there was no evidence that the young prince had any Axis connections, he had, after all, been educated in Germany; it was prudent to keep a "fatherly eye" on him. [44]

Although in law the sultanate was not a British protectorate, but a sovereign state in alliance with Britain, the India Office wanted total control of foreign relations. The British, of course, had long considered the entire gulf their lake. This attitude was emphasized in a 1933 address to Arab shaikhs by the political resident in the Persian Gulf who sought to justify policy with the assertion that the British were the guardians of tribal peace. "We have saved you from extinction at the hands of your enemies." he proclaimed. [45] Insofar as concerned Oman, the British resented even the most minor indication of the sultan's independence. In 1937, Sultan Said planned a trip to Europe and Japan. Without consulting the British, he wrote a letter to President Franklin D. Roosevelt, saying that he wanted to include the United States in his itinerary. The American minister in Iraq, Paul Knabenshue, had visited Muscat in 1934 to deliver a letter from Roosevelt to the sultan, marking the one-hundredth anniversary of the Treaty of Amity and Commerce between the United States and the sultanate. Roosevelt liked the idea of receiving the ruler of Muscat, Oman, and Dependencies. [46]

Meanwhile, Knabenshue discussed the sultan's proposed visit to Washington with the British ambassador in Baghdad, who had no advance knowledge of the sultan's intentions. Knabenshue was surprised that the sultan would propose such a visit without first consulting the British government. The American minister resident in Baghdad informed the State Department that it was not in the best interest of the United States to invite the sultan to Washington unless the British approved. Secretary of State Sumner Welles agreed. While in law Muscat-Oman was an independent country, in practice the sultanate was under British protection. Secretary Welles suggested to the president that the State Department informally discuss the sultan's proposed visit with British Ambassador Sir Ronald Lindsay.[47] When Ambassador Lindsay learned about Sultan Said's letter to the American president, he immediately informed London. Lindsay speculated that the sultan was up to no good, that his proposed trip might be a cover for a visit to Rome to plot with Mussolini's fascists.[48] Lindsay's opinion did not deter the president, who enjoyed the prospect of receiving the sultan and, ignoring the opinion of his advisors, issued the desired invitation.[49]

The India Office was not concerned about an Omani-Italian connection. After the Italian invasion of Abyssinia, Sultan Said had expressed his displeasure. According to Bushire, the sultan was "obviously trying to have it both ways, using His Majesty's Government when it is to his advantage, and disregarding them when it suits him."[50] The India Office instructed Muscat to tell the sultan that in view of the close relationship between the Sultanate of Oman and His Majesty's government, London hoped that the sultan would, in the future, share all communications with foreign governments.[51] The sultan refused. The sultanate and the United States were linked by treaty. Washington and Muscat had a historic connection, and the sultan had written to President Roosevelt immediately after his election to the presidency. In addition, the sultanate did not "want to inconvenience the British Government with any communication but those which we consider ought to go through them."[52]

After traveling to Japan to visit his father, the sultan sailed to California and than traveled to Washington, where he arrived on 3 March 1938. He was received at Union Station by a reception committee led by the secretary of state. Prior to the sultan's arrival, the National Museum informed the White House that one of the sultan's predecessors had sent camels, blooded horses, silk rugs, and several shawls to President Martin Van Buren. The rugs and shawls were now included in the museum's collection.[53] The president was also briefed about the sultanate, which according to the State Department had a population of approximately 500,000. American trade with Muscat was infinitesimal, but a few Omani dates and a little dried fish entered the American market. In addition, the Singer Sewing Machine Company maintained a small office in Muscat. An American missionary presence too continued in the sultanate; The Arabian Mission of the Dutch Reformed Church had small hospitals in both Mutrah and Muscat, and a clinic at Birka. Roosevelt was also informed that the British political agent in Muscat exercised considerable influence both regarding the internal and the foreign affairs of the sultanate. "It is understood, however, that the present Sultan is somewhat sensitive in the matter of British control and is inclined to become increasingly assertive on the point."[54]

The State Department described the Omani ruler as small in stature, and well dressed, a man of considerable dignity, who was both shrewd and energetic and had a good sense of humor. At the same time, Sultan Said was considered easy to converse with, and extremely polite. It appeared likely that the sultan would mention two issues in his conversations with the president, oil exploration and the revision of the Treaty of 1833 that placed restraint on his power to levy duty on goods coming from the United States into the sultanate. The State Department noted that Washington had earlier signified willingness to negotiate a different treaty, one that would grant the sultanate unconditional most-favored-nation status. In 1930, London had discussed with Washington the economic problems faced by the sultanate and had asked if the United States would consent to waive its rights under the treaty of 1833 and permit Muscat to raise the tariff on American goods entering the sultanate. Although Washington had no objection to an increase in tariff rates, the U.S. Constitution prohibited amending the treaty. Hence, a new treaty was necessary. Washington had been prepared to negotiate a new treaty with Muscat, but the British had not pursued the issue. As for oil, American oil companies were active in the Arabian Peninsula. Standard Oil Company of California located an important find on the Island of Bahrain and was also engaged in operations in Saudi Arabia. Not long before, the sultan had asked Standard Oil Company to investigate petroleum possibilities in his territory, but such activity could pose difficulty with the British in light of the 1923 agreement between Britain and the sultan's father, in which the ruler agreed not to permit exploitation of his petroleum resources without the consent of the government of India.[55]

As it turned out the sultan's visit did not result in any sort of substantive agreements; it was essentially a social visit. Americans pursued their economic interests, but Muscat was so very far away, located in an area that was clearly recognized as a British sphere. The result of the sultan's visit was pleasant memories, a new book for the Omani ruler, and a handsome dagger for the American president.[56]

Although Sultan Said frequently appreciated British assistance, throughout his reign he remained frustrated by his dependence. A letter in 1937 from a member of the royal family Sayyid Mohammed Said, to the political agent in Muscat reported in confidence that the sultan had been in contact with Shaikh Isa bin Saleh and Shaikh Sulaiman bin Himyar, discussing the possibility of the new treaty with the tribes of the interior. According to Sayyid Mohammed Said, the sultan complained about British interference and wished for an alliance with the Omani people in order to strengthen his position against Britain. The sultan asked Shaikh Isa to recognize him as the ruler of both Muscat and Oman. Shaikh Isa replied that as long as Imam Mohammed bin Abdul-Khalili was alive, he could not abandon him. A note from a British official who read the letter suggested that its author, Sayyid Mohammed Said, was famous for inventing news. At the same time, the letter might very well contain some truth.[57]

Sultan Said wanted more control at home, but he did not want involvement in events outside his territories. He showed little interest in the neighboring Arab states and no interest in Arab issues beyond his borders. When the Peel Commission, authorized by London to investigate conflict in Palestine, suggested in 1937 a partition plan that would have divided a portion of the country between Arabs and Jews, the sultan raised no objection. He said that it was out of the question to expel either Arabs or Jews from Palestine. Since the two groups could not live together in harmony, partition was the only solution.[58] Then in January 1938, when the sultan received an invitation to attend a proposed Arab national conference in Bludan, he would not attend, nor would he send a representative. According to the sultan, he was much too busy looking after the welfare of his own people to meddle in the Palestinian conflict. Palestine was not his affair, nor was it the concern of any other Arab state.[59]

Regardless of his desire for independence, the sultan accepted the inevitability of depending on the British for defense. British officers led the Muscat Levies. Reporting on the condition of the levies in 1938, their commander, A.C. Byard, at the end of his tour of duty in Muscat, expressed satisfaction with the changes that had taken place during the previous two years. The men who served at the beginning of 1936 had not been adequately clothed or equipped. Many had been deficient in drill and manual; not one could do a fair route march. In addition, the men lacked blankets and winter clothes, and lived in barracks that were not weather proof. Many men died as a result of poor living conditions. There were no medics to treat the sick or injured. Pay was meager and social life non-existent. The levies were a dumping ground for former slaves and their relatives. Commander Byard instituted changes during the winter of 1936. Warm clothes and medical care were provided. Later a canteen and a farm with a dairy were established. Byard ordered the merchants, who had kept the men in debt, away from the camp. Prior to his departure he suggested that in the future local Baluchis be recruited for the levies, men who had resided in the sultanate at least two years and who had an interest in the country.[60]

Concerned about the growing threat of the Axis powers, as World War II approached in the spring of 1939, the British wanted to strike a bargain with the sultan: in exchange for re-arming and training his troops, London wanted the right to use Omani waters and Omani ports during the struggle with fascism that now appeared inevitable.[61] The sultan, of course, was worried with the security of his country. He considered both the possibility of a foreign power attacking by sea and the possibility of tribal unrest on land. He relied on the levies for the defense of Muscat and Mutrah, which were protected by only a few policemen and a small palace guard.[62] Despite improvements that had earlier increased the morale and improved the training of the Muscat Levies, difficulties remained. An Indian officer in charge of the levies reported serious doubts about both the fighting quality and the integrity of the sultan's soldiers. Old rifles entrusted to the levies at Bait-al-Falaj were continuously stolen and sold to visiting Bedouin from the interior.

The sultan requested that the British maintain a plentiful reserve of ammunition at Bait-al-Falaj. He said that he wished to purchase a large quantity of arms and ammunition from England in the event that enemy agents stirred up unrest among the tribes in the interior. In addition, he planned immediately to mount one of his three-pounder guns on Fort Mirani in preparation for a possible attack by sea. In Muscat, Captain Hickinbotham suggested that the sultan was hoping "to kill two birds with one stone," and the British were to be a part of his stone. Hickinbotham advised the political resident that it was the time to come to an understanding with Sultan Said about the position he would take in the event of war.[63] Meanwhile, British officers examined Fort Mirani. The stoneworks were in good condition, but the towers were crumbling and would be very expense to repair. The sultan discarded the idea of mounting guns on the fort.[64]

Discussing the importance of the sultanate, the Foreign Office told the Admiralty at the beginning of August 1939 that Britain could never allow the Muscat coast to fall to a non-Arab or major Arab power. If any power threatened the sultan's territory, Britain would have to defend it "as vigorously as if it were directed against a part of our territory." But the matter was not a simple one. During the conflict which appeared to be approaching, areas of lesser strategic importance might have to be abandoned in favor of areas of greater strategic importance. If London guaranteed to defend the sultan's territory, the sultan could very well call on the British to fulfill that guarantee at the wrong moment.[65] No guarantee was issued. Nevertheless, in September, at the outbreak of hostilities, the political resident called on the sultan to inform him that Britain and France were at war with Germany. The sultan was repelled by the Axis powers. He had no sympathy with either their methods or their goals, and he was not interested in using the opportunity to distance himself from Britain. Sultan Said immediately expressed his readiness to render such assistance as was within his power.[66]

Once again the world was engulfed in a major war and after the fall of France in June 1940, Italy joined the Axis powers. The southeastern region of Arabia was not removed from strife. Fascists, both German and Italian, were prominent in neighboring Yemen, and Italy controlled Ethiopia. "It is difficult to recapture the feeling of danger which hovered over the Red Sea coastlands in those years when Mussolini's schemes were in the ascendant."[67] The British were engaged in a battle, not only for an empire, but for their very survival. Oman was an important strategic asset. As ruler of a sovereign state, Sultan Said bin Taimour did all that was within his capacity to fulfill his promise of support. The sultanate did not declare war on the Axis powers, but he wholeheartedly cooperated with the war effort; three air bases were established on his territory; his ports and harbors were open to the British navy.

NOTES

1. Bertram Thomas, *Alarms and Excursions in Arabia*, London: Allen & Unwin, 1931, p. 143.
2. Michael Field, the Merchants, Woodstock, N.Y.: Overlook, 1984, pp. 185-186.
3. Thomas, p. 127.
4. Ibid., p. 117.
5. Vincenzo Maurizi, *History of Seyd Said*, London: Oleander, 1984, p. 101.
6. Report, Muscat, April 1929, CO732/37/4/ XC/2107, Public Records Office, (hereafter cited as PRO.)
7. Ibid., September,1929, CO732/37/4/ XC/2107, PRO.
8. Ibid., October 1929, CO732/37/4/ XC/2107, PRO.

8. Ibid., October 1929, CO732/37/4/ XC/2107, PRO.

9. Letter, Political Agent to Political Resident, Muscat, 30 May 1930, India Office Library (hereafter cited as IOL).

10. Letter, Randolph to Secretary of State, Baghdad, 29 March 1924, (hereafter cited as NA).

11. Letter, 26 May 1926, 890a. 6363, NA.

12. Letter, Hosman to Randolph, Muscat, 26 February 1924, 890a. 6363, NA.

13. Letter, Bremner to Sultan, Muscat, 12 December 1932, IOR/15/6/145. IOL.

14. W. Harold Storm, *Whither Arabia,* London: World Dominion Press, 1938, p. 66.

15. Ibid., p. 89.

16. Sir Ronald Wingate, *Not in the Limelight,* London: Hutchinson, 1959, pp. 88-89.

17. Ibid., p. 90.

18. Ibid., p. 81.

19. Monthly Report, Muscat, 1929, CO732/37/4/ XC/2107, PRO.

20. Ibid., pp. 28-29; Oddly, it was not until August 1929 that the American consul in Baghdad reported to Washington on British interest in the possibility of oil in Oman. He had received reports about the Geological Survey of 1925 and told the State Department that the prospects of finding oil in large enough quantities appeared poor, and also that the British consul in Muscat had not treated the geologist differently than the American missionaries. He had denied the geologist permission to visit the interior. As a result, their survey had been limited to the narrow coast line.

21. G.J. Eccles, "The Sultanate of Muscat and Oman" in *Journal of the Royal Central Asian Society,* 1927, pt. 1, p. 24.

22. Ibid., pp. 40-41.

23. Telegram, Political Resident to Foreign Secretary, Bushire, 26 October 1928, PRO.

24. Ibid., 1 November 1928, PRO.

25. Telegram, Political Resident to Political Agent, Bushire, 25 October 1928, CO 732/36/5 XC 002136, PRO.; Telegram, Political Resident to Government of India, PRO.

26. Telegram, Political Resident to Foreign Secretary, Bushire, November 1, 1928, PRO.

27. Telegram, Viceroy to Political Resident, November 5, 1928, PRO.

28. Letter, Political Resident to Government of India, Bushire, 7 November 1928, PRO.

30. Letter, Randolph to Secretary of State, Baghdad, 2 August 1929, 890a. 248/1, NA.

31. Letter, Biscoe to Foreign Secretary, Government of India, Bushire, 12 January 1931, R/15/6/53, IOL, pp. 1-2.

32. Letter, Fowle to Biscoe, Karachi, 8 September 1930, R/15/6/53, pp. 1-4, IOL.

33. Letter, Biscoe to bin Turki, Bushire, 16 September 1930, Biscoe to Foreign Secretary, Government of India, Bushire, 12 January 1931, R/15/6/53, IOL.

34. Letter, bin Turki to Biscoe, Dehra Dun, 6 October, 1930, R/15/6/53, IOL.

35. Letter to Fowle, Bushire, 20 October 1930, R/15/6/53, IOL.

36. Letter, Biscoe to the Foreign Secretary, Government of India, At Sea, 12 November 1930, R/15/6/53, pp. 1-3, IOL.

37. Ibid., pp. 6-10, Biscoe to Foreign Secretary, Government of India, Bushire, 12 January 1931, R/15/6/53, IOL.

38. Letter, Biscoe to Foreign Secretary, Government of India, Bushire, 12 January 1931, R/15/6/53, IOL.

39. Letter, Plumptree to Fowle, Karachi, 10 May 1931, R/15/6/53, IOL.

40. Memorandum, Fowle to Political Resident, Karachi, 12 May 1931, R/15/6/53, IOL.

41. Letter, Caroe to Fowle, New Delhi, 21 January 1936, IOR/15/6/217, IOL.

42. Letter, Special Branch to Intelligence Bureau, Singapore, 29 January 1936, IOL.

43. Letter, IIquay to Consul General, Istanbul, 23 May 1940, IOR/15/6/230, IOL.

44. Letter, Hay to Inspector-General of Police, Bushire, 21 September 1942, IOR/15/6/230, IOL.

45. Address by the Political Resident in the Persian Gulf, 23 September 1933, IOR/15/16/224, IOL.

46. Letter, Sultan to President, Muscat, 20 March 1937, Franklin D. Roosevelt Library Library, Hyde Park, New York (hereafter cited as FDRL), and Letter, Roosevelt to Sultan, Washington, 16 June 1937, FDRL.

47. Letter, Welles to Roosevelt, Washington, 11 June 1937, FDRL.

48. Telegram 1746, Secretary of State for India to the Foreign Office, London, 27 June 1937, IOR/15/6/2/3, IOL.

49. Letter, Roosevelt to Sultan, Washington, 16 June 1937, FDRL.

50. Telegram, British Consul to Secretary of State for India, Bushire, 1 July 1937, IOR/15/6/2/3, IOL.

51. Telegram 1854, Secretary of State for India, to Political Resident, London, 10 July 1937, IOR/15/6/2/13, IOL.

52. Letter, Sultan to Political Agent, Muscat, 21 August 1937, IOR/15/6/2/13, IOL.

53. Memorandum, Washington, 1 March 1939, FDRL.

54. Memorandum, Washington, 19 February 1938, FDRL.

55. Ibid.

56. Letter, Roosevelt to bin Taimour, Washington, 2 May 1938, FDRL.

57. Letter, Sayyid Mohammad Said to the Political Agent, Muscat, 3 November 1937, IOR/15/6/236, IOL.

58. Letter, Political Agent, to Political Resident, Muscat, 23 July 1937, IOR/15/6/379, IOL.

59. Letter, Political Agent to Political Resident, Muscat, 11 January 1938, IOR/15/6/379, IOL.

60. Report, Byard, 1938, IOR/15/6/385, IOL.

61. Letter to Gibson, London, 5 June1939, IOR/15/6/385, IOL.

62. Telegram, Hickinbotham to Political Resident, Muscat, 12 June 1939, IOR//15/6/385, IOL.

63. Telegram, Hickinbotham to Political Resident, Muscat, 15 July 1939, IOR//15/6/385, IOL.

64. Telegam, Hickinbotham to Political Resident, Muscat, 19 July 1939, IOR//15/6/385, IOL.

65. Telegam, Foreign Office to Jarrett, London, 1 August 1939, IOR/15/6/385, IOL.

66. Telegram 435, Political Resident to Secretary of State for India, Bushire, 4 September 1939, IOR/15/6/385, IOL.

67. Freya Stark, *Dust in the Lion's Paw,* London: Arrow, 1990, p. 21.

3

ENEMIES: OLD AND NEW

The years immediately following the end of World War II were marked by dramatic political and economic changes in the Middle East. Britain had emerged from the war victorious, but on the verge of bankruptcy. Immediately after victory, the British people went to the polls and rejected their gallant war leader, Winston Churchill. The new Labour party government in London was prepared to recognize the necessity of giving up vast portions of the British Empire, even the most precious jewel in the crown, India. When the British departed from India, in 1947 two states -- Hindu India and Moslem Pakistan -- achieved independence. At the same time, the British government decided to relinquish its mandate for Palestine. Unable to resolve the conflicting demands of Arabs and Jews, London turned to the United Nations. The United Nations adopted a partition plan that divided Palestine between Arabs and Jews. The Arab states, which were members of the world body, united in opposition and vowed to destroy the newly created state of Israel. The failure of Arab armies to achieve victory in 1948 resulted in an escalation of frustration directed against the United States, which had supported Israel, the European powers that had dominated the Arab world, and the traditional Arab rulers who had long cooperated with western powers.

The failure of Arab arms in Palestine led to the 1952 military coup in Egypt that forced King Farouk into exile and resulted in the ascendancy of Colonel Gamal Abdul Nasser. The new Egyptian leader wished to build a modern independent nation-state. In 1954, President Nasser concluded an agreement with Britain that required the withdrawal of all British troops from Egypt. The agreement, however, provided that in the event of an attack by an outside power, British troops could return to protect the Suez Canal. Two years later, Nasser nationalized the canal. Without consulting the United States, Britain and France worked out a plan with Israel to topple Nasser. Hence, Israel invaded Egypt; the British and French airlifted troops into the Canal Zone to protect the canal. Despite the cold war and the two opposing alliance systems that it had spawned -- the North Atlantic Treaty Organization led by the United States and the Warsaw Pact controlled by the Soviet Union -- Moscow and Washington stood together to condemn the attack on Egypt. As a result, Nasser prevailed. He emerged as a hero, his prestige enhanced in his own country and throughout the Arab world.

The Suez campaign was yet another blow to British prestige. In the decade of the 1950s British authority clearly continued to decline, but Britain, a shadow of the great power that had previously dominated the area, remained an important presence in the Gulf, protecting the region that supplied the oil necessary for the western allies. Sultan Said took no pleasure in Britain's descent. Both Nasser and communism were anathema to the sultan. He detested Nasser's Arab nationalism and was repelled by the Egyptian leader's growing dependence on the Soviet Union. Sultan Said continued to rely on British support to counter his old adversaries, the Saudis, and to provide assistance against Omani tribes in the interior. At the same time, the sultan looked to the British to assist in safeguarding the sultanate against his latest enemies, communist ideology and Arab nationalism.

After the Allied victory, two Royal Air Force bases continued operations in Muscat-Oman, one in Salalah, the other in Masirah. In addition, the Royal Navy maintained a base at Khorquwai. Although Britain no longer ruled India, considering a possible Soviet threat and the likelihood of rich oil deposits, London wanted to insure the continuation of the British relationship with the sultan and with the other gulf rulers. The British Political Residency, now in Bahrain, was responsible for dealing with ten Arab shaikhdoms on the western shore of the Arab Gulf as well as with Muscat-Oman. Together with the shaikhdoms, Muscat-Oman remained outside the current of world politics, indifferent to the Arab League, unresponsive to events in Palestine, and untouched by communism. Sir John Troutbeck in Cairo suggested in April 1948 that the situation was unlikely to last. As a result of radio, the beginning of education, and the impact of western capitalism, the Arab awakening was spreading to the small kingdoms on the gulf. He concluded: "Whatever may be the feelings of one or two petty chiefs, the urge for independence from western rule is surely bound to grow even in the little Arab states in the Gulf."[1]

In the immediate postwar period the people of Muscat-Oman focused on economic issues. Oil had not yet been discovered in the sultanate. Economic opportunities were few, but prices rose, including the price of rice, the staple of the local diet, which did not grow in Oman and had to be imported. In order to reduce the high cost of living, in 1948 the sultan introduced newly minted baizas and fixed their rate of exchange at 200 to the Maria Therese dollar and 100 to the Indian rupee. Political Resident Sir Rupert Hay doubted that these measures would be effective. The vast majority of Muscat's merchants were foreigners, "an unprincipled crew" not interested in local needs, but only in making money quickly. They exported essential commodities, which earned higher prices in other gulf states or in Pakistan. Hay wanted the sultan to impose some measure of export control.[2] In the following months, large quantities of Japanese piece goods reached Muscat from Aden and Colombo. As a result, the price of Indian piece goods fell and Muscat merchants lost money.[3] At the same time, large quantities of gold were smuggled past Muscat customs agents and delivered to ports in India and Pakistan. The gold was made into "rough ornament," worn by Baluchi women whom the smugglers provided with passports. "It is quite a usual sight to see poor women on the deck of the ships wearing ornaments that suggest considerable wealth."[4] Given the lack of economic opportunity in the sultanate, many tribesman left to obtain employment in neighboring states. By the summer of 1949, every day approximately fifty Omani left for the oil fields of Kuwait and Bahrain.[5] At the same time, isolated from the outside world, those who remained in the interior of Oman steadfastly maintained their traditions and their independence.

The Muscat government considered how to increase agricultural production. In 1950, one foreign expert after inspecting the Batinah coast, suggested that if pumps to lift water were utilized inland from the existing palm belt, it would be possible to provide an additional zone for growing fruits and vegetables, products that would be purchased by the oil companies active in the region. The sultan's government planned to establish an experimental farm near Sohar.[6] But the sultan appeared to be less concerned with agriculture than with his prestige. In 1950, Sultan Said asked that in official documents the title "His Highness" not be used. Although he had not said so out loud, British officials perceived that as an independent ruler, the sultan wished to be called "His Majesty." If London began to refer to the sultan as "His Majesty," it was likely that the shaikhs of Kuwait and Bahrain would want the same title. At this juncture, Whitehall had no intention of calling any Arab Gulf ruler, "His Majesty." According to the Foreign Office, "Kings and Emperors alone, by virtue of their pre-eminence in the monarchical hierarchy, assume and are accorded the title of Majesty." London suggested that if Sultan Said wanted to be called "Majesty," he could proclaim himself king, or even emperor of Muscat. Since Muscat-Oman was an independent country, what the sultan decided to do in this matter, an internal affair, was not the business of the British government.[7]

The sultan remained the only gulf ruler who had direct relations with foreign powers. Nevertheless, together with the other gulf rulers, he was interested in maintaining his traditional ties with the British. Although before World War II the sultan had emphasized his American connection by visiting the White House, Political Resident Sir Rupert Hay reported in January 1949 that "there is no sign of any inclination to turn to the USA in place of His Majesty's Government in spite of the display of American strength and wealth in the Gulf." During the month of Ramadan, July 1948, the U.S.S. *Greenwich Bay* commanded by Captain W.S. Butt called at Muscat. The sultan did not consider the visit official; the authorities showed no interest in entertaining the crew, and Sultan Said was reluctant to receive the American captain.[8] The following year in August, the ship returned to Muscat. The sultan noticed that when the *Greenwich Bay* fired the salute, the ship did not fly the state flag. The sultan asked his minister of foreign affairs unofficially to inform the captain. Although Sultan Said may have been indifferent to the American naval presence on this occasion, the British were grateful for the presence of the American ship. Crew members repaired the agency's broken air-conditioning unit.[9] Anglo-American relations in the gulf region, however, were not always pleasant. From the close of World War II tensions that had developed between the two English-speaking nations during the war increased. London welcomed Washington's interest in the Middle East but at the same time wanted to maintain Britain's dominant political and commercial position in the area. Although both the British and American leaders realized that discord between them would benefit the Soviet Union, disputes over oil concessions and aviation rights resulted in antagonism.[10] When a group of American senators visited Bahrain in 1949, they called on the political resident;   in the course of conversation, their chairman remarked that "the United Kingdom was finished, that 20 million of its inhabitants want to migrate to South Africa." [11]

Meanwhile, remote from his people, the sultan marked time, hopeful that the old imam who controlled the tribes of the interior would soon die so that he would have the opportunity to fill the vacuum and assert his authority in Nizwa. The imam did not cooperate;   often reported near death, he continued miraculously to recover and carry on his activities. Waiting for the appropriate opportunity, Sultan Said turned his attention in 1948 to a tract of land at the northern end of Oman that bordered on the Trucial Coast shaikhdoms. He opened a road suitable for automobile traffic through the Wadi al Jizzi. [12]   But travel through the desert remained risky. It was inadvisable to travel the road without security provided by the sultan. [13] A surgeon, attached to the British consulate, Captain Mathews, in November 1949, traveled to Bait-al-Falaj to look after the Muscat infantry. Returning to the capital by truck, he was threatened by a camel driver carrying a rifle. Fortunately, two soldiers in the back of the truck leaped out and seized the rifle. Friends of the camel driver joined the action. The British prevailed. The camel driver who pointed his rifle was arrested and handed over to the local wali.   Apparently, the camel driver feared the truck would frighten his camels.   The consul advised that in the future considerable caution was necessary when approaching camel caravans. All vehicles were warned to come to a complete halt a considerable distance from a caravan. [14]

Concerned with opinion in the conservative interior, the sultan attempted to eliminate the possibility that his enemies might accuse him of failure to protect Islam. In 1947, Sultan Said, had ordered the American Mission school closed. Then in June 1948 he issued a degree prohibiting the importation and sale of liquor. At the same time, he unofficially permitted some liquor for the use of the Christian community, making a special exemption in favor of the British, and he later agreed that all Europeans and Anglo-Indians be permitted a reasonable quota. The sultan, however, refused to put the exemption to the ban on liquor in writing, preferring that it remain a gentleman's agreement;   Sir Rupert Hay, assumed that the term "European" included Americans. He did not, however, clarify the point with the sultan because the only American residents in Muscat were missionaries, who abstained from all alcoholic beverages. [15] Meanwhile, "many of the local wine-bibbers began stocking their cellars with whatever they could lay their hands on at any price."[16] When word reached Sultan Said that some of his relatives were avoiding the ban by drinking alcoholic beverages with the Europeans at the Cable and Wireless Club, he attempted to restrict social intercourse between members of his family and the Europeans in Muscat. Earlier the sultan had received a letter from the imam complaining that foreigners were beginning to interfere in Oman. The imam instructed the ruler to remember that religious interests should take precedence over material considerations.[17] Pressure from religious authorities continued to increase. In the summer of 1949, Minister of the Interior Sayyid Ahmed bin Ibrahim, wanted the sultan to impose a number of new restrictions on his subjects. Bin Ibrahim wanted smoking on the streets, rejoicing at weddings, and short sleeves for women prohibited. The sultan agreed.[18]

Administration did not interest Said bin Taimour, which was unfortunate because most of his appointed walis were inexperienced, lacked education, and had no access to outside experts. Despite good intentions, they often failed to gain the confidence of the people. Occasionally the sultan personally visited some of the tribal shaikhs, but Hay complained that the ruler generally remained aloof. Realizing that he needed administrative assistance, in 1941 Sultan Said told the British that he wanted to hire a competent Englishman whom he could designate Minister of Foreign Affairs. This person would in effect run the administration, conduct relations with the consulate, supervise customs, and during the sultan's long periods in Dhofar "to all intents and purposes rule Muscat on his behalf."[19] It was difficult to find the right candidate for the position. The climate in Muscat was unfavorable, amenities were limited, which indicated that a bachelor would be a better candidate than a married man, a bachelor young enough to respect his seniors and not clash with the political agent in Bahrain. The salary offered by the sultan was modest, and there was no guarantee of job security beyond the initial three-year contract. The Foreign Office suggested that to find the proper candidate the sultan would have to sweeten the deal, offer a higher salary and an air-conditioned house.[20] In the spring of 1948, the Foreign Office was still looking for the right man. Hay had a long talk with the sultan in July and told him that it would be difficult to spare a suitable Foreign Office official. The sultan agreed to settle for a former Indian Political Service Officer, even if he had no experience in the Arab Gulf, but only on condition that the candidate was willing to learn Arabic.[21] Finally, in October 1948, the sultan appointed an able British officer, Lt. Colonel Basil Woods-Ballard as minister of foreign affairs.[22] Some members of the royal family were not pleased. The sultan's unhappy uncle, Sayyid Shahab, who had often assumed the sultan's duties when Sultan Said was absent from Muscat, showed his displeasure by leaving for India.[23]

Although lacking an interest in administration, the sultan was keenly concerned with progress in oil exploration. Petroleum Concessions Limited sent geologists to Dhofar in March 1948. The geologists found no indication of oil, a bitter blow for the sultan. Depressed, he insisted that if the company did not intend to operate in Dhofar it give up the option it had earlier obtained and permit other firms to take over its concession. A former member of the Indian Political Service who had previously served as political agent at Muscat, Major Richard Bird arrived in Muscat in May 1948 to act as liaison officer for Petroleum Concessions Limited. He reported to the sultan that the company had paid a considerable sum to the Al Bu Shamis and the Na'im tribes in return for permission to explore parts of the interior for three years with a provision that if necessary the company could extend exploration for an additional two years. The sultan was angry. He objected to direct negotiations between the company and the tribes.

At this juncture, some of the Buraimi tribes declared that they were not ruled by the Sultan of Muscat and that any negotiations about oil on their territory had to be negotiated directly with them.[24] Shaikh Saqr Bin Sultan of Buraimi broke with tradition and did not come to see the sultan. Although the sultan was confident that Shaikh Saqr Bin Sultan would not assert total independence, Bird was worried. His job was to find oil, and it would be much easier if Sultan Said controlled all of his territory, without opposition from either tribal shaikhs or religious leaders.[25] Hay reported to Foreign Secretary Ernest Bevin in December 1948 that the longer the imam lived, the better the sultan's chances. Once tribesmen in the interior saw neighboring territory prosper as a result of oil company activities, they were more likely to refuse another imam and turn to the sultan. Muscati merchants were already dreaming of the fantastic fortunes they would make when oil was discovered in commercial quantities. By the end of 1948, the sultan made peace with Bird, and Political Resident Hay was confident that during the winter months the oil company would be able to carry out considerable exploration without "arousing the Sultan's resentment."[26]

It appeared that as a result of oil exploration, a large number of westerners might in the future enter the sultanate; a ten-year-old treaty between London and Muscat that confirmed the British right to extra-territorial jurisdiction, a right first granted in 1839, was to expire in February 1951. [27] The sultanate was the last sovereign state to permit Britain that privilege. Under the treaty, the court of the British political agent exercised jurisdiction over all British subjects in Muscat. Clearly, extra-territoriality was outmoded, a relic of the past. If London insisted on preserving the right, the government might offend the Middle Eastern countries that wanted Britain out of the Arab Gulf. Possible criticism from India, Pakistan, and from the Soviet bloc was also a concern. In addition, "certain elements" in the United States would disapprove. Despite the disadvantages of pressing to maintain extra-territoriality, London was reluctant to give up jurisdiction over British subjects. Whitehall considered Muscat's courts to be uncivilized. According to the Foreign Office, "the retention of extra-territoriality may obviate friction and criticism arising from the subjection of Europeans to a primitive and inappropriate legal system." There was also the possibility that relinquishing extra-territorial jurisdiction would reduce British prestige in the gulf, and that the Saudis would consider it yet another indication of British weakness. [28]

The sultan and the British reached a compromise, the new Treaty of Friendship, Commerce and Navigation, which was not concluded until December 1951, abolished extra-territorial jurisdiction, but an exchange of letters between the two parties provided for recognition of the British consul general's authority over British nationals in the sultanate. In addition, the treaty provided British financial assistance for the employment of British officials in the administration of the sultanate, and for the recruitment of British officers into the sultan's army, the Muscat Levies. [29]

Meanwhile, financed by British interests, the explorer Wilfred Thesiger, known to the Arabs as Mubarak bin London, had arrived in October 1945 at the Royal Air Force camp near Salalah. The men stationed there were not permitted to visit the town or travel outside their camp's perimeter without Omani escort. Arabic-speaking Thesiger entered the wali's palace in Salalah to obtain permission to travel. The portly wali wore a large dagger on his waist. He was dressed "in a white shirt reaching to the ground, a brown cloak embroidered with gold, and a Kashmiri shawl which was loosely wrapped around his head." Although Thesiger wanted only a small party to accompany him on his journey across the desert, the wali insisted that the explorer needed at least forty-five men. Concerned with the cost of the expedition, Thesiger convinced the wali to compromise. He took thirty men. From Salalah Thesiger and his Arab party set out to explore Southern Arabia.[30] The following year, in October 1946, the Englishman returned to the sultanate to continue his odyssey, crossing the Empty Quarter from Mughshin to the Trucial coast before returning to Salalah. Recognizing that the sultan was unlikely to permit a foreigner into an area controlled by the fanatical imam on this journey Thesiger avoided asking for the wali's permission.[31]

Later Thesiger explored Omani territory from October 1949 until the following April. He explored from the Trucial coast west of the Hajar Mountain and down to the coast opposite Masirah. According to Thesiger, south of Ibri the imam from Nizwa maintained law and order, but north of Ibri the tribes "acknowledge no overlord and nobody feels safe. Abductions into slavery are carried out even from tribal villages."[32]

Knowing that the sultan would object to Thesiger's movements into the interior of the sultanate, the Foreign Office had agreed to his departure without consulting Sultan Said. London justified Thesiger's explorations with the unlikely excuse that British officials could do little to stop him, and, after all, the shaikhs in the interior might be susceptible to overtures from the American oil company Aramco, which operated in Saudi Arabia. From his own sources, the sultan learned about Thesiger's activities and ordered his visa canceled. Thesiger was not deterred; with British approval he entered Oman from the Trucial coast.[33] Passing out gifts, Thesiger moved south. He wanted to enter the Jebal Akhdhar. Here he was stopped by the imam, who opposed permitting an infidel to enter his territory and ordered the Duru and other Ibadhi tribesmen to hold all of the passes.[34] Finally, British officials informed Thesiger that the sultan was angry and he had to leave.[35]

Returning to London in April 1950, Thesiger called at the Foreign Office to report on his explorations. He said that the tribes in both the southwest and northwest of the Jebel Akhdar had no loyalty to the sultan; they followed their imam, whose territory likely contained oil. The xenophobic followers of the imam opposed a Wahhabi presence as much as they opposed a Christian appearance. As a result, they would stand against the Saudis, but also against the sultan, and were unlikely to admit any oil company. The geologist advised that the best policy to follow would be to put "the whole of the central area (between the Hugf and the Bani Kitab) in cold storage for a few years." The imam was an old man. His successor was likely to be younger; however, exclusion of outsiders might very well continue. As for the possibility that Sultan Said would be elected imam, Thesiger said that it "was wishful thinking on the sultan's part." Turning to the area around Buraimi, the explorer warned that the tribes located there did not have allegiance to the sultan or to the imam and might very well turn to Ibn Saud. There was also an area in the Liwa, the location of the Bani Yas tribe, which appeared to be open to American penetration. Thesiger heard rumors that Americans had visited Liwa and moved further northeast into Abu Dhabi territory.[36] American competition was a concern. In February 1949, the sultan had consented to British exploration into Buraimi, but local shaikhs refused to cooperate with the British party, maintaining that they were not the sultan's subjects. The Foreign Office feared the possibility that the Buraimi shaikhs might sign a concession with an American oil company. If this happened, the sultan would protest and the result might lead to friction between Washington and London.[37] The Saudis used the independence of the interior to their advantage. Prior to the discovery of oil, there were no fixed borders between kingdoms in the vast stretches of Arabia. After Saudi Arabia awarded an oil concession to the American company Aramco in 1933, the company requested precise information on the dimensions of its concession. The Buraimi Oasis region posed a major difficulty. In an area of approximately 100,00 square kilometers, which controlled access to the coast via Wadi al-Jizzi, the Dhahirah, Oman, and the Trucial coast, five different tribes lived in nine villages claimed by the Sultan of Muscat, Oman and Dependencies, the Shaikh of Abu Dhabi, and the King of Saudi Arabia. The matter of boundaries was not immediately resolved. In 1949, Saudi Arabia claimed sovereignty over Buraimi and announced that the borders would not be negotiated with Muscat, but with the imamate. Then the Saudis, who had controlled the oasis in the ninetieth century prior to their eviction in 1869 by the Sultan of Muscat, once again in August 1952 occupied Buraimi.[38] The British had earlier speculated that some of the tribes in the region would willingly pledge allegiance to the Saudis because they were attracted by Saudi gold.[39]

The sultan, of course, wanted the Saudis out. The British agreed. Negotiations to settle the dispute began. The United States was an interested party, and London was concerned about American public opinion in the event that Britain decided to use military force to end Saudi control. Sir Bernard Burrows told the Foreign Office that a limited number of sophisticated Americans realized that Saudi Arabia was a medieval kingdom ruled by a despot; however, Saudi Arabia was an important source of American oil, and most Americans viewed the conflict as one between a small country and imperialist Britain.[40]

Washington recommended arbitration. Britain agreed after Whitehall reluctantly concluded that in the event of military action against the Saudis, Riyadh would complain to the United Nations, and the British position in the Arab Gulf would be open to critical public examination.[41] Meanwhile, interested in undermining the Saudi claim to the oasis, the British intercepted two letters that implicated the Saudis in the slave trade in Buraimi.[42] At the same time, Sultan Said saw an opportunity to unite Oman and strike at the Saudis. Tribes loyal to the imam were willing to join forces with the sultan's men to evict the Wahhabi. As the tribes rallied to the sultan, the British intervened to halt the proposed military action, and the sultan lost an opportunity.[43]

Finally, arbitration talks began in Geneva in September 1955. London nominated its former minister in Teheran, Sir Reader Bullard, to the tribunal to act as arbitrator on behalf of both Abu Dhabi and Muscat-Oman. Riyadh appointed Deputy Foreign Minister Shaikh Yusuf Yasin to act as arbitrator on behalf of Saudi Arabia. The British and Saudi arbitrators jointly appointed additional arbitrators. At the second meeting of the tribunal, the leading counsel for the British government claimed that transgressing the arbitration agreement, Saudi agents in the disputed area were paying bribes to win support. Witnesses were called to confirm the British charge. In response, the Saudi arbitrator, Shaikh Yasin, called a witness to refute the charges. After listening to the proceedings, Sir Reader Bullard concluded that the Saudi arbitrator was not fulfilling his mandate, that he made no attempt to act impartially and had coached the witness. As a result, Sir Reader declared that the tribunal could not reach a judicial conclusion. The only step consistent with his independence and honor was to resign. Other members of the tribunal also resigned. At this juncture, the British lost patience and used military force to expel the Saudis from Buraimi. Riyadh did not accept defeat. The Saudis requested United Nations supervision in Buraimi or another attempt at arbitration. London refused.[44] The sultan and the ruler of Abu Dhabi, Shaikh Shakhbut, in December 1955 met in Buraimi to greet assembled dignitaries and celebrate victory with a breakfast banquet that included sheep and buzzard.[45]

But the issue of the final status of the territory remained unresolved. Saudi Prime Minister, Prince Faisal in November 1955 stated:

As a result of the British armed aggression and forcible occupation of the Buraimi region, and in view of the fact that the British government justifies this armed aggression on the basis of its agreements with the Sultan of Muscat and the Sheikh of Abu Dhabi, His Majesty's Government in Saudi Arabia reasserts its full rights in that region and refuses to recognize any concessions that have been, might be, or shall be granted in the Buraimi region for any purpose to anybody, be it an individual, a company, or a government, without the consent of the Sa'udi Arabian Government.[46]

In addition to trouble in Buraimi, once again the sultan faced difficulties with tribes in the interior. Imam Mohamed had died in May 1954. His successor, Ghalib bin Ali, disregarded the thirty-four-year-old Agreement of Sib and claimed independence from the sultan. Protecting the sultan's territory, the British at the end of 1955 provided air transport and technicians to put down the rebellion. Ghalib bin Ali was defeated. With the sultan's permission, he retired to a remote village. Because the deposed imam's brother, Talib bin Ali, was not satisfied, he left Oman for Saudi Arabia. With Saudi encouragement, bin Ali raised a force to liberate Oman. Assisted by the leader of the Beni Riyam tribe, Sulaiman bin Himyar, in the summer of 1957, Talib entered the sultanate at the head of a rebel force, which quickly achieved control of central Oman. Once again the sultan asked for British help. The Royal Air Force came to his rescue and the sultan regained most of his territory. At this juncture, however, the rebel leaders did not leave the country, but instead retreated to Beni Riyam territory, the inaccessible Jebel Akhdar massif. The rebels continued to receive assistance -- weapons, ammunition, and money -- from Saudi Arabia. In addition, some Saudi subjects joined the rebel forces. Egyptian President Gamal Abdul Nasser too encouraged the rebels. As a result of the resources available to him, Talib became more confident and his forces began to shell government camps in the interior. The sultan did nothing at all. He did not like the capital Muscat, and spent most of his time in the remote province of Dhofar, confident that the British would protect his interests.

London was concerned: "Whatever the theoretical legal position, we are regarded in the Gulf and indeed generally as protecting Muscat and failure to do so would have repercussions elsewhere."[47] A large British operation in the sultanate so soon after the disastrous Suez crisis was certain to attract unwanted attention at the United Nations, and a negative reaction in Washington. Prime Minister Harold Macmillan later wrote in his memoirs that after 1956 "to embark single-handed upon a further military enterprise, even of a modest character, seemed at first to some of my colleagues hazardous and even foolhardy."[48] But two years after Suez, British interests were at risk and London did not opt out. The British government was ready to use military force and simultaneously fend off attacks on the diplomatic front. In July 1957 Macmillan wrote to President Dwight D. Eisenhower, requesting American tolerance for British military involvement in the sultanate. He noted that both the Saudis and the Egyptians were encouraging the Omani rebels, that the sultan was a true friend of the West and needed support. In his reply to the prime minister, the president mentioned that rumors had circulated in London to the effect that American oil companies, intent on damaging British oil concessions in the region, played a role in fueling the rebellion. Eisenhower declared that such rumors were completely false, that "too great a readiness on our part to criticize each other for whatever troubles we may encounter in our dealings with other nations will harm efforts to solve our common problems."[49]

After earlier failing to convince the Security Council to consider the "armed aggression of the United Kingdom against the independence, sovereignty and territorial integrity of the Imamate of Oman," ten Arab states, in December 1957, asked the General Assembly of the United Nations to put the question of Oman on its agenda. The Special Political Committee held hearings. A representative of the imamate argued that the 1920 Treaty of Sib confirmed Oman's status as an independent state. Speaking on behalf of the sultan -- the Sultanate was not a member of the United Nations -- the British responded that the Treaty of Sib had not ended the sultan's sovereignty, that the matter was an internal affair, and outside interference in the internal affairs of the sultanate was contrary to the United Nations' charter.[50]

The British continued to provide the sultanate with military assistance. In the spring of 1958, Lieutenant R.F. Gray serving in Oman with the Royal Marines, recorded his impressions. The British troops endured the heat in May -- daytime temperatures of 120 degrees -- with an abundant supply of water from springs and streams, and a ration of whiskey from the local oil concession. They ate tinned food, fresh eggs, and scraggy chickens. Mail and beer were airlifted to the troops. Gray praised the tribesmen who volunteered to serve the sultan, especially the Bedouin who made keen soldiers. These men did not understand English, but were trained to act on orders spoken in English. They treated their weapons carefully and loved to shoot. However, they considered shooting a sport, and it was sometimes difficult to convince them to take it seriously.[51]

British assistance in crushing the rebels appeared to many Arabs to be yet another example of traditional imperialism. An Arab wrote to the *Economist* in the summer of 1957, saying:

> Britain could have served the interests of the British people and humanity best had it demonstrated its power in support of the national uprising of the peoples of Oman, and the other territories of the Persian Gulf protectorates who have been struggling alone against the despotic and feudalist regimes of their countries.[52]

At the same time, the political resident in Bahrain advised the Foreign Office that defeating the rebels in the Jebel Akhdar would not end opposition to the sultan. In order to maintain the loyalty of his subjects, the sultan would have to change his style, become more accessible to his people and agree to spend money on projects that would benefit the population.[53] The British considered development programs for the sultanate. They pressed for programs that would have an immediate psychological impact on the adult population, projects to improve health, build roads, develop agriculture.[54]

Immediately after World War II, London had attempted to convince the sultan to open schools to provide the skilled workers that would be essential for the development of his territories. His negative response to educating his subject was incomprehensible to some foreign office officials and others in the Arabian Department. But the sultan did not like change and equally abhorred both communism and Arab nationalism. He maintained that academic education would produce a generation demanding political transformation and hence endanger both the traditional system and the British position:

> Where could the teachers come from? They would come from Cairo and spread Nasser's seditious ideas among their pupils. And what is there here for a young man with education? He could go to the university in Cairo or to the London School of Economics, finish in Moscow and come back here to foment trouble.[55]

In Muscat, Consul-General Major Leslie Chauncy discussed the importance of inaugurating some changes that would satisfy the people. He suggested the formation of a council of shaikhs. The sultan said no. He ruled according to the Koran, personally. The establishment of a council was against custom. The sultan agreed to continue to consult each shaikh about his tribe and any matter that was directly related to his area, but a formal council was out of the question. Sultan Said refused to recognize the need for modernization. He insisted that the present rebellion was rooted neither in a desire for improved living conditions, nor was it motivated by nationalism. The rebellion was simply the work of a few individuals who craved power. Compromise with them was impossible because they had both Egyptian and Saudi support.[56]

Meanwhile, as a result of successful Royal Air Force attacks on the Jebel, families moved into caves, and food was in short supply. The British pressed the sultan to permit shaikhs willing to intervene to communicate with rebel leaders. After negotiation with the shaikhs rebel leaders agreed to recognize the sultan's suzerainty, but they were unwilling to leave the mountains. As a result, at the end of October 1958, the RAF launched a heavy attack. Although the rebel tribesmen were illiterate, for two weeks after the attack RAF planes dropped leaflets calling for an end to the uprising. Intermediaries moved up and down the mountain, trying to achieve the same result. Neighboring Arab rulers had little sympathy for the sultan. From the Trucial states, Shaikh Saqr told the British that Sultan Said was hated throughout the sultanate, that perhaps, with British assistance, he would now achieve victory. However, he would not be able to hold onto his territory. Nevertheless, Shaikh Saqr volunteered his services as mediator between the sultan and the rebels. Regardless of the sultan's reputation, London was committed to ending rebel activity. Hoping to avoid negative publicity, Britain secretly dispatched additional troops to Oman. The Foreign Office was concerned that Washington would learn about the escalation of British military activity and that the State Department would react negatively. Hence, Secretary of State John F. Dulles was informed.[57]

When the rebellion was finally quelled in February 1959, the Foreign Office once again attempted to convince the sultan to introduce change. Among the suggestions offered was that he tour his domains, show himself to his people. Queen Elizabeth was presented as a model. Her Majesty enjoyed her country estate at Balmoral and sometimes retreated there. However, the queen limited the time she spent away from London. After a queen limited the time she spent away from London. After a brief absence she returned to her capital and showed herself to her people. At the same time, the British suggested that the sultan work out some sort of accommodation with Saudi Arabia, although London cautioned against arbitration warning, "We had tried that once before and it had been rendered impossible by Saudi bribery." In victory the sultan was not forgiving. Prior to the end of the rebellion, he had agreed to aid the former rebels, whose gardens and irrigation systems had been destroyed. Once the rebels were defeated, he changed his mind and ordered that they receive nothing. At the same time, he canceled an amnesty for surrendered rebels, an amnesty that he had earlier ordered.[58] The sultan's vindictive behavior was well-known and even extended to the those who were already imprisoned. When political prisoners in Jalali Fort became seriously ill, Colonel David Smiley, who had been seconded from the British army, asked the sultan's permission to move them to the missionary hospital in Mutrah. The sultan replied that he preferred they die in prison and that they die sooner rather than later so that he would have more room at the fort to imprison others.[59]

The British were concerned with the steady barrage of propaganda directed against the sultan. Cairo Radio in 1959 continued to broadcast messages supporting the imamate and conveyed the impression that most of Muscat-Oman was in revolt against the sultan. The Foreign Office wanted the British Broadcasting Corporation (BBC) to counter the Cairo broadcasts by providing factual information from the sultanate. The BBC asked for information about the date harvest, fishing, pearling, trade with India, Zanzibar, and other countries. In addition, the broadcasting company wanted as much as possible about the military situation. The BBC also requested any sort of information about schools, irrigation, the work of Development Secretary, Colonel Hugh Boustead, and "any plans the Sultan had for developing the country."[60] The sultan, during a visit to London in September 1959, called at the Arabic Service of the BBC to look into the possibility of establishing a broadcasting station in Muscat. There were, of course, numerous stumbling blocks to broadcasting from the sultanate. Concerned with offending conservatives, the sultan resisted the British suggestion that he agree to broadcast music. There was also the question of technicians to operate the station and radio sets to pick up the broadcasts. The British speculated that a member of the royal family would have to be associated with the station, technicians could be hired from Pakistan, and radio sets might be distributed to Omanis either free or at minimal cost.[61] Finally, the sultan, still uncertain that a broadcasting station was necessary, at last took a tentative step forward in 1961 by ordering a small transmitter.[62]

Resistance to change remained the sultan's policy. Surrounded by a small circle of trusted advisers, he shot at tunny fish jumping out of the water in the vicinity of his palace and devoted time to the study of astrology. Before making important decisions, he consulted books on numerology, maintaining that such books were of considerable assistance.[63] He appeared to be indifferent to the steady exodus of his subjects, and to the suffering of those who remained in the Sultanate. Sultan Said kept a watchful eye on his enemies, old and new. He held fast to his traditional policies, continued to placate conservatives, to rely on Britain, and to refrain from spending money.

NOTES

1. Letter, Troutbeck to Burrows, Cairo, 8 April 1948, FO 371/68319/XC 2329, Public Record Office, (hereafter cited as PRO).

2. Report, Hay to Foreign Office, Bahrain, 1948, FO 371/68319/XC 2329, PRO.

3. Ibid,. 1949, FO 371/74937/XC2329, PRO.

4. Intelligence Report, November 1949, Muscat, FO 371/74936/XC2329, PRO.

5. Intelligence Report, Andrew, Muscat, August 1949, FO 371/74938/XC 2329, PRO.

6. Letter, Hay to Waterlow, Bahrain, 31 January 1950, FO 371/82093 XC001650, PRO.

7. Minute, London, 11 March 1949, PRO.

8. Annual Report, Hay to Bevin, Bahrain, 21 January 1949, FO 371/74935/XC2328, PRO, and Letter, Hay to Bevin, Bahrain, 8 June 1949, FO 371/74989/XC 2329, PRO.

9. Report, Muscat, August 1949, FO 371/74938/XC 2329, PRO.

10. Robert Hathaway, *Ambiguous Partnership*, New York: Columbia University 1981, p. 217.

11. Report, Muscat, August 1949, FO 371/74938/XC 2329, PRO.

12. Report, Hay to Foreign Office Bahrain, 1948, FO 371/68319/XC 2329, PRO.

13. Letter, Bird to Ellison, Muscat, 14 November 1948, FO 371/68318/XC 2329, PRO.

14. Intelligence Report, Chauncy, Muscat, November 1949, FO 371/74938/XC 2329, PRO.

15. Hay to Bevin, Bahrain, June 1948, FO 371/68318/XC 2329, PRO.

It appears that serving in the Middle East influenced the political resident's style. He signed his letter to Foreign Secretary Bevin, "I have the honor to be with the highest respect, Sir, Your most obedient humble servant."

16. Report, January 1949, Bahrain, FO 371/74935/XC 2329, PRO.

17. Letter, Bird to Ellison, Muscat, 14 November 1948, FO 371/68318/XC 2329, PRO.

18. Report, Muscat, August 1949, FO 371/74938/XC 2329, PRO.

19. Letter, Hay to Bevin, Bahrain, 17 April 1948, FO 371/68318/XC 2329, PRO.

20. Letter, Troutbeck to Burrows, Cairo, 8 April 1948, FO 371/68319/XC 2329, PRO.

21. Letter, Hay to Burrows, At Sea, 8 July 1948, FO 371/68318/XC 2329, PRO.

22. Report, Hay to Bevin, Bahrain, 21 January, 1949, FO 371/74935/XC2328, PRO.

23. Report, Muscat, November 1949, FO 371/74936/XC 2329, PRO.

24. Annual Report, Hay to Bevin, Bahrain, 21 January 1949, FO 371/74935/XC2328, PRO.

25. Letter, Bird to Ellison, Muscat, 14 November 1948, FO 371/68318/XC 2329, PRO.

26. Letter, Hay to Bevin, Bahrain, 6 December 1948, PRO, and Report, January 1949, Bahrain, FO 371/74935/XC 2329, PRO.

27. Letter, Burrows to Hays, Bahrain, 28 September 1949, FO 371/74962 XC001336, PRO.

28. Note, Furlonge, London, 31 October 1950, FO 371/82148 XC 001605, PRO.

29. John Marlowe, *The Persian Gulf in the Twentieth Century*, New York: Praeger, 1962, p. 196.

30. Alfred Thesiger, *Arabian Sands*, London: Penguin, 1991, p. 43.

31. Ibid., p. 76.

32. Report, May, 1949, FO 371/74937/XC 2329, PRO.

33. Minutes, March 1950, London, FO 371/82123/XC 001605, PRO.

34. Note, Hay, Bahrain, 29 March 1950, PRO.

35. Thesiger, p. 329.

36. Record of a visit to Eastern Department by Thesiger, London, 12 April 1950, PRO.

37. Memorandum, Sind London, 14 March 1949, FO 371/74973/XC 001336, PRO.

38. Calvin H. Allen, Oman, *The Modernization of the Sultanate*, Boulder: Westview, 1987, pp. 112-113.

39. Minute, Buckmaster, London, 5 January 1952, FO 371/104316/EA 1081/1143, PRO.

40. Letter, Burrows to Ross, Washington, 31 December 1952, FO 371/104274, PRO. No mention, of course, that the sultan too was a despot.

41. Telegram 1512, Foreign Office to Bahrain, London, 23 December 1953, FO 371/104371, PRO.

42. Letter, Residency to Eastern Department, Bahrain, 15 December 1953, FO 371/104316/EA 1081/1154, PRO.

43. Neil McLeod Innes, *Minister in Oman,* London: Oleander, 1987, pp. 21-22.

44. Alexander Melamid, "The Buraimi Oasis Dispute," in *Middle Eastern Affairs,* Vol. 7, 1956, pp. 61-63.

45. Innes, p. 167.

46. Quoted in Aziz Sahwell, "The Buraimi Dispute" in *Islamic Review,* April 1956, p. 17.

47. Quoted in Miriam Joyce Haron, "Britain and the Sultan of Muscat and Oman and Dependencies," in *Diplomacy and Statecraft,* March 1993, pp. 91-92.

48. Ibid., p. 90.

49. Miriam Joyce, "Washington and Treaty-Making with the Sultan of Muscat and Oman" in *Middle Eastern Studies,* January 1994, p. 146.

50. Allen, p. 113.

51. Letter, Pritchard to Lucas, London, 24 July 1958, FO 371/132872/EA 1673/3, PRO.

52. Quoted in Morroe Berger, *The Arab World Today,* New York: Anchor, 1964 pp. 297-298.

53. Haron, p. 93.

54. Letter, Foreign Office to Man, London, 8 November 1961, FO 371/ 156818/XC 164523, PRO.

55. Quoted in J.B. Kelly, *Arabia, The Gulf and the West,* New York: Basic Books, 1980, p. 119.

56. Haron, p. 93.

57. Ibid., pp. 94-95.

58. Ibid., p. 96.

59. Minute, Walmsely, London, 14 August 1958, FO 371/132903/EA 1944/34, PRO.

60. Letter, Waterfield to Bullock, London, 14 September 1959, FO 371/140215/7634, PRO.

61. Letter, Man to Beaumont, Bahrain, 2 December 1959, FO 371/311/14021/7236, PRO.

62. Report, Muscat, 1961, FO 371/156758/XC164523, PRO.

63. Note, Beaumont to Stevens, London, 10 August 1959, FO 371/140292 XC 187509, PRO, and Minute, Middleton, London, 27 August 1959, PRO.

4

RELINQUISHING GAWADUR

Although Sultan Said bin Taimour moved slowly and cautiously, he did acquiesce to one important change in the decade after the Second World II; he yielded the Omani territory of Gawadur to Pakistan. In the cold war competition that dominated the politics of the era, Pakistan remained committed to the western camp. Encouraged by the United States, the government of Turkey concluded an agreement with Iraq in 1955 for consultations about the defense of the Middle East. The arrangement, known as the Baghdad Pact, was extended to include Iran, Britain, and Pakistan. Three years after the establishment of the pact, in February 1958, Egypt and Syria merged under Egyptian President Nasser to form the United Arab Republic (UAR). A month later, the sultan's neighbor, Yemen, joined the UAR. Nasser -- at least on paper -- had virtually stretched down to reach Sultan Said's border.

Arab nationalism appeared to move from success to success. A bloody military coup in July 1958 overthrew the Hashemite Kingdom of Iraq, striking a blow at the heart of the Baghdad Pact. Fearing the complete collapse of the pro-Western governments in the Middle East, Washington dispatched marines to Lebanon, and London sent troops to Jordan. Given Nasser's accomplishments, the British had no wish to antagonize Pakistan and supported what they considered a reasonable transfer of territory from the sultan to Karachi. But the sultan did not easily part with his only overseas possession. His agreement to do so was a tribute to British diplomacy and yet another indication that the British government continued to play an important role in the Middle East.

As the result of tribal warfare, at the end of the eighteenth century the Sultan of Muscat had been forced to flee his country; the Khan of Kalat, whose lands included Gawadur, presented the port to the sultan. The boundary between Gawadur and neighboring Kalat State had not been defined. In 1946 the Government of India prescribed a presumptive boundary, giving Muscat an arc with a twenty-mile radius around Gawadur. The area was populated by Hindus, a wealthy Agakhani community, and Baluchi tribesmen. The British did not share information about this newly drawn boundary with either the sultan or the khan.[1]

After the partition of India in 1947, the old Indian province of Mekran, which once had included Gawadur, acceded to Pakistan. The government of Pakistan tried unsuccessfully to dispute the sultan's claim to the Gawadur, which covered an area of 300 square miles and contained a population of approximately 12,000 inhabitants. The area was composed of a narrow strip of plain, parallel with the Baluchistan coast, and connected with it by a low tract of sand approximately a quarter of a mile across, forming two large bays. The plain sloped on the seaward side almost to sea level, but ended landward in a row of cliffs. The sultan controlled Gawadur through an Arab wali and an Indian administrator.

The Political Agent in Muscat, Major Stewart, in March 1948 discussed Gawadur with Sultan Said. Major Stewart said that Kalat State wanted to buy Gawadur. The sultan replied that he was bound by treaty not to cede any part of his territory, except to the British government. He understood that, of course, Kalat might attempt to take the territory by force. If he lost the territory as a result of aggression, the world would recognize that he had behaved honorably, but selling territory handed down by ancestors was incompatible with honor. Major Stewart warned that some sort of political maneuvering was taking place between the Nawab Bai Khan Gichki, who the government of Pakistan had recognized as the leader of Mekran State, and the khan. Both, of course, wanted Gawadur to be in Pakistan. The sultan said there was little he could do; the acting wali in Gawadur was inexperienced but he had no one else to send.[2]   In 1945 the sultan had asked for the loan of a British administrator for Gawadur. No suitable officer was available; an Indian official from Baluchistan took the position. The administrator arrived in Gawadur in 1947 and introduced a rationing system, which failed as a result of opposition from the wali, the Baluchi

headmen, and the sultan's customs official, who for their own purposes diverted much of the allotted quotas of cloth and food.[3]
    In January 1949, British Consul in Muscat, R. Elden Ellison, visited the province and reported his impressions of Gawadur's cliffs, which he said were "broken in places into fantastic shapes; one spur is strongly reminiscent of Exeter Cathedral." Consul Ellison visited the small town at the base of the cliffs. Because the bay was shallow, he was taken from his British India steamer by one of the native crafts that regularly brought passengers to shore. The British agent, Rashid Ahmed, the principal British residents, and a Boy Scout band greeted Ellison. The Boy Scouts played "a rather bedraggled version of 'God save the King." This reception made him feel "a little like the embarrassed Englishman in General John Regan who insists that he is not the Lord Lieutenant."[4] Ellison toured Gawadur in a truck, which was the only motor vehicle in the province. He was entertained by the Indian community and visited their school open to boys and girls with separate classes for each. Funds for the school came from the Aga Khan, who was revered by his followers. Ellison was impressed "by the attempt to maintain education and civilization on a very modest scale in this out-of -the-way spot."[5] A later visitor to Gawadur, Minister of Foreign and External Affairs Neil McLeod Innes also commented on the school and the schoolmaster's pleasure in the achievements of his students, both boys and girls.[6]
    Ellison enjoyed his eventful visit to Gawadur. He was entertained by native dancers and touring female impersonators from Karachi. As a result of the British consul's presence, departing from convention, the wali attended the show. Ellison said that the population appreciated his going there and recommended that notwithstanding the difficulty of arranging transportation to Gawadur the consul in Muscat be authorized to visit annually.[7] His recommendation was accepted and visits from officials in Muscat became routine.[8]
    London, however, considered the area an awkward foreign enclave in Pakistani territory. Britain had no oil interest in Gawadur. The Burma Oil Company had abandoned its option on the development of Gawadur oil resources in 1939 and had no desire to return. At the same time, the chiefs of staff reviewed the strategic value of the territory as a landing field for the Royal Air Force. The chiefs decided that the Gawadur base was too small to be practical, and hills 1,300 feet high only four miles from the landing area were an impediment to expansion. As a result, the chiefs of staff wanted simply to retain the rights in Gawadur given to the RAF under a 1946 civil air agreement. As

was the sentiment in Karachi, the British favored separation of
Gawadur from Muscat, cessation of Gawadur to Pakistan.
Discussion continued. The sultan developed a strong bias
against Pakistan. He attempted to exclude Pakistanis from
employment in Muscat, giving preference to Indian Muslims,
Christians, or Hindus. He also refused to sell a parcel of land in
Gawadur that the Pakistan director general of posts and
telegraphs wished to acquire. The sultan agreed to give title to
the land to the British government, but not to the Pakistani
authorities.[9]

In February 1949, Political Resident Sir Rupert Hay
doubted that the mostly Baluchi population objected to the
sultan's domination of Gawadur and said that in the unlikely
event of a plebiscite, nearly all would vote to remain under the
sultan. According to Hay, successive sultans had ruled Gawadur
without difficulty for almost 170 years. Recalling that he had
served in Baluchistan between 1942 and 1946 and visited other
ports on the Mekran coast, Hay said that Gawadur compared
favorably with other areas, including Pasni and Ormara then in
Pakistan. Nevertheless, despite his prediction that once
transferred to Pakistan prosperity in Gawadur would decline,
Hay admitted that from the "ideological point of view" the
contemplated transfer was sensible. Hay recommended to
Secretary of State Ernest Bevin that he be authorized to tell the
sultan that Gawadur was naturally a part of Mekran and
continued Omani control might lead to agitation against Arab
rule.[10]

Meanwhile, Foreign Office officials reviewed several
international agreements pertaining to the sultanate. A 1862
Anglo-French agreement pledged both London and Paris
"reciprocally to respect the independence" of the Sultan of
Muscat, and an 1891 agreement between Britain and the sultan
provided that no territory belonging to Muscat "would be sold,
leased or ceded to any country except the United Kingdom."
Prior to World War 1 Britain had used the 1862 agreement to
force the sultan to revoke the cession of a piece of land he had
presented to France for a coaling station. One Foreign Office
official remarked that a post World War II British government
taking similar action, "would be regarded as exceptionally high-
handed."[11]

The British government had assured France in 1913 that
the Declaration of 1862 remained binding. The Foreign Office
considered whether or not acquiescing to the cession of Gawadur
without consulting the French would violate the terms of the
1862 agreement. Consulting the French, however, might

embarrass Paris since France was then engaged in resisting Indian claims to French controlled territory. Since French interest in Muscat "has for years dwindled and has now almost vanished," it appeared unlikely that Paris would object to cession. The Foreign Office decided to abstain from discussing the issue with the French government. In the unlikely event that the French protested their exclusion from the matter, the British were confident that they could explain that their motive was to protect France from embarrassment.[12]

Sultan Said visited Pakistan at the beginning of December 1949. The Pakistanis tried to discuss with him their desire to obtain the territory, but the sultan was not interested.[13] Whitehall informed the Pakistanis in July 1950 that London was unwilling to pressure the sultan to relinquish what was his only overseas territory. Meanwhile, prior to the partition of India, Baluchis from Mekran had been recruited for the Muscat infantry. According to Political Resident Hay: "They were as good material as could be obtained for the Muscat Infantry." After Mekran acceded to Pakistan, these men became Pakistani nationals but continued service in the Muscat infantry where the language of drill was not Arabic, but Urdu. On the evening of 27 September 1950 some Baluchi soldiers mutinied. Thirty Pakistani nationals attacked a guardroom to release three of their friends who had been sentenced to detention. A lieutenant who attempted to intervene was pushed aside. The Baluchis settled down on the hockey field and refused to return to their barracks or to give up their liberated friends. Colonel Woods-Ballard was convinced that other Baluchi infantrymen in the ranks supported the rebels. Leslie Chauncy advised that the men be told that since they were dissatisfied serving in Muscat, they would be discharged immediately. If they agreed to leave quietly, they would be paid and repatriated at government expense. Ninety Baluchis left Muscat by steamer via Gawadur. Given the growing tension between the sultanate and Pakistan, it was no longer prudent to recruit such troops.[14]

Pakistan continued to raise the Gawadur issue, and in April 1954 suggested that the question could be settled if the sultan would agree to a lease in perpetuity. The British government prepared a draft lease that the Pakistanis approved. At the beginning of January 1955, the Foreign Office instructed Political Resident in the Persian Gulf Sir Bernard Burrows to deliver the draft lease to the sultan and explain that "the Pakistanis may make trouble if he rejects the proposal. H.M.G. considers that it would be in the Sultan's interests to agree to this lease."[15] Sultan Said was not prepared to accept the lease arrangement unless London agreed to participate. British participation would insure that the Pakistanis paid the required rent. Whitehall did not want to have to dun the Pakistanis for rent "possibly for 99 years." As a result, London told the sultan that Whitehall could not participate in the proposed lease or accept responsibility for collecting the rent.[16]

Without British participation, the sultan rejected the lease arrangement. The Foreign Office returned to the possibility of arranging for the sale of Gawadur. At this point, Sultan Said did not yet have revenue from oil and Whitehall speculated that although he had previously rejected the idea of selling the territory, if the purchase price was high enough he might now be willing.[17] The British agreed to continue pressing the sultan to sell Gawadur. At the same time, Whitehall told Pakistan to make a generous offer, before the sultan had the funds that the sultanate's oil resources would surely produce.[18] British Consul General in Muscat Major Leslie Chauncy cautioned Burrows that the sultan "drives a hard bargain and will not be hustled." Chauncy also emphasized that the sultan wanted all discussions to remain secret until the conclusion of negotiations, and that if at any stage the possibility of leasing or selling Gawadur leaked to the public, he would not proceed. According to the sultan, "his was not a people's government and it was not his policy to consult his subjects before taking decisions."[19] Nor apparently was it his policy to confide in his ranking civil servant. The sultan's minister of foreign and external affairs, Neil McLeod Innes, who in 1953 had replaced Woods-Ballard, visited Gawadur and "all in good faith" announced that the ruler had absolutely no intention of ceding the port to Pakistan.[20]

Meanwhile, the Foreign Office was concerned that the Pakistanis might lose patience with diplomacy and resort to force.[21] The Pakistanis told the British that their intelligence service had learned that the Indian government was trying to lease Gawadur from the sultan. They warned that Karachi would regard the lease or sale of Gawadur to India as an unfriendly act.[22] This accusation had first been made in 1949, when the Pakistani government claimed that British officers were encouraging the sultan to work out some sort of arrangement with India.[23] London found no evidence to support the Pakistani claim, which the Commonwealth Relations Office called "quite baseless and indeed ridiculous."[24]

The high commissioner for Pakistan in London, Mohammed Ikramullah, called on the director of the Commonwealth Relations Office, Sir Gilbert Laithwaite, on 6 June 1955 to discuss Gawadur. He stated that a majority of the people living in that province would welcome a direct association with Pakistan, that his government was anxious to conclude the matter, and that he had been appointed a plenipotentiary with full powers to conduct negotiations with the sultan. Pakistan wanted possession of Gawadur either by sale or lease. Laithwaite suggested that the Pakistanis concentrate efforts on purchasing the territory and that if an offer to purchase was made, it be "as generous as possible" and "as soon as possible." Ikramullah said that his government was prepared to make such an offer of up to £ 1.5 million. Laithwaite called the figure too low. The sultan was likely to demand between 2 and £ 3 million. Sir Gilbert told Ikramullah that he had personal experience negotiating with the sultan who was "an extremely capable negotiator, very tough and particularly interested in matters of finance." Ikramullah requested assistance, including a British presence at any future discussions held between the sultan and the Pakistanis. Laithwaite assured Ikramullah that the Foreign Office was willing to help.[25]

During a visit to London in July 1955, Sultan Said agreed to see the Pakistani ambassador, but not to start discussions with him, or even consider the issue until he returned to Muscat. The Omani ruler did, however, hint that he was attracted to the idea of setting a price for Gawadur. However, he wanted the offer to reach him via the British. Whitehall considered it best that the two parties negotiate directly; if that was impossible, London would act as an honest broker.[26] Sir Bernard Burrows discussed terms. He suggested that the sultan lease the territory for a short period, perhaps five years, with the understanding that at the end of the lease the territory would be sold to Pakistan.[27] Afterwards, British officials discussed the issue with the Pakistani high commissioner. Upon learning of these discussions, the sultan expressed alarm. The British attempted to reassure him, explaining that he had insisted that the Pakistanis deal through Whitehall. Hence, "we could hardly avoid discussing things with them; indeed, it was obviously to his advantage that we should know what they had in mind." The sultan wanted time to think the matter over.[28] He later said that on security grounds he did not want the Gawadur issue discussed on the telephone.[29]

Pakistani Prime Minister Chaudhri Mohammed Ali, complained in August 1955 that Gawadur was the center of a large smuggling operation. He was determined to stop smuggling. To accomplish his goal, it was necessary to put up a customs cordon. Since Gawadur had been a gift to Muscat from Kalat, the inhabitants were Pakistani. Such a cordon would set

Pakistani against Pakistani. The prime minister urged the British
to move quickly on the Gawadur issue. [30]
United Kingdom High Commissioner in Karachi Sir
Alec Symon called the Gawadur issue, "potentially inflammable"
and warned that the Pakistanis might be "very unpleasant."
Symon suggested that the sultan make a deal while Pakistan
remained "in a mood to be generous." [31] The English-language
Karachi newspaper *Dawn* on 27 September 1955 published an
article about Gawadur by London correspondent Nasim Ahmed,
who reported that large quantities of contraband goods were
smuggled into Pakistan from Gawadur, causing a serious loss of
revenue. Ahmed wrote that the British government unjustly
upheld Muscat's right to Gawadur because London was
interested in oil and its strategic position in the Gulf. Ahmed
further stated that in the dispute over sovereignty, the Pakistani
foreign office had a serious disadvantage. Pakistan lacked
experienced diplomats and London withheld essential documents
from Karachi. The article predicted that the Pakistani
government would receive total support from the people in an
effort "to restore Pakistan's sovereignty over this port." [32]
Discussing the Gawadur issue three days later, High
Commissioner Ikramullah appeared to be conciliatory. He was
willing to consider a special position for Muscatis in Gawadur,
and in the event that after relinquishing the territory the sultan
decided to visit, he would be received with special honor. [33] The
sultan, however, was in no hurry either to visit Gawadur or to
make a decision about the future of the province. London
continued to express concern about the possibility of a Pakistani
military takeover of the territory and warned that it would be
extremely difficult to restrain the Pakistanis. [34] Meanwhile, the
Pakistani press again took up the issue. One inflammatory
article indicted the British for not doing anything to resolve the
problem, for "always leaving Pakistan in the lurch." It also cited
the fact that almost all the officials in Gawadur were Arabs, and
claimed:

> Some Arabs, particularly those from the Persian
> Gulf states, are usually born smugglers. Be it
> diamonds or gold, opium or hashish (charas),
> limousines or unimportable silks, one can count
> on a particular type of Arab to deliver them.
> Operating from Gawadur, with the help of the
> local Mekrani population, they have coolly
> deprived the Government of Pakistan of scores
> of rupees in import duties. [35]

Reviewing the situation in November, the Foreign Office noted that unlike other gulf rulers, the sultan of Muscat was an independent ruler. He did, however, lean heavily on British support and had steadfastly refused to negotiate with the Pakistanis except through London. Nevertheless, the Foreign Office was still unable to convince the sultan to sell Gawadur. The sultan professed "to fear the verdict of posterity if he traded away his ancestral rights." Meanwhile, according to the Pakistanis, it was only Britain's special position vis-a-vis Muscat that restrained them from military action. Karachi complained that the British were not truly doing their best to support their cause.

Here was a dilemma for the Foreign Office. Although favoring secession of the territory, London did not want to antagonize the sultan. [36] There was still no progress on the Gawadur question when the British focused their attention in November 1955 on crushing the rebellion led by the Imam of Oman. [37] British officials in Karachi warned that if news of British supported operations against the imam reached Pakistan before an indication of movement on Gawadur, anti-British hostility would rise and Pakistan might move into the coveted territory. [38]

Whitehall linked the rebellion and the question of Gawadur. The area controlled by the imam was in the vicinity of oil deposits explored by the Iraq Petroleum Company. London feared that British assistance in putting down the rebellion would be interpreted by the Arab world as yet another indication of western imperialism, and because no progress had been made on the Gawadur question, Pakistan might use the occasion to lash out against both London and Muscat. [39] Sir Bernard Burrows visited the sultan in Salalah during November. Although he was not optimistic about the outcome, the political resident was determined to press the ruler to agree to negotiate some sort of lease-sale arrangement. Burrows warned Sultan Said that action against the rebels would result in an international outcry against the British use of force. Therefore, the ruler was obligated to London "to purchase such support as is possible for our efforts to represent his cause abroad." [40] After "arduous discussion" and a long list of conditions, Sir Bernard earned the sultan's agreement in principle to a lease-sale arrangement. The ruler asked for £ 5 million and because Gawadur might contain oil, he wanted an arrangement to share whatever oil was found. Moreover, any documents that were signed by the two parties had to be witnessed by Britain. Further, the sultan insisted that a portion of an agreed upon payment be made in dollars. Previously,

Oman had benefitted from the expertise of Pakistanis working in the sultanate. Recently, perhaps as a means of applying political pressure, Karachi had postponed sending men to fill essential positions in the Muscat forces and administration. Now the sultan also wanted an agreement by Pakistan to provide technical personnel when needed in Muscat. The sultan also asked for an undertaking by Pakistan to give the same priority to Muscat's rice requirement as to those of any other country. Above all, Sultan Said desired to avoid the word "sale" in a future public statement. Burrows reported victory to London; the sultan had finally agreed to accommodate Pakistan. Sultan Said had been swayed by his reliance on British advice and "wish to help them internationally."[41]

Pakistani Prime Minister Chaudhri Mohammed Ali protested that "the sultan was opening his mouth too wide in suggesting five million pounds." But Pakistan was ready to bargain. Prime Minister Ali understood that the rebellion against the sultan in the interior of Oman required a delay in a final resolution of the Gawadur question. At the same time, he did not know how to prevent negative publicity in Pakistan, where British action against the rebels in Oman appeared as a further indication of western imperialism.[42]

Meanwhile, the Pakistani High Commissioner in London complained that Britain never did enough for Pakistan. Foreign Secretary Lord Alec Douglas Home met with High Commissioner Ikramullah on 14 December. According to Ikramullah, the Pakistanis needed evidence that the United Kingdom recognized her true friends. Pakistan wanted ships, two destroyers, immediately. Pakistan was involved in a confrontation with India and needed support. A recent Russian visit to Kashmir was evidence that India had a powerful friend, while Pakistan, loyal and western in her outlook, had not even words of comfort from her allies and especially the United Kingdom. After venting his frustrations, Ikramullah expressed confidence that the Gawadur issue would be resolved, and he did not anticipate serious reaction against the sultan or London.[43]

At the end of the year, the Gawadur question remained unresolved. Despite earlier suggestions that the government in Karachi would accept the sultan's terms, the Pakistanis refused to include a reference to oil in the agreement. It appeared that negotiations had collapsed.[44] Although the British wanted to resolve the issue, 1956 was a very difficult year for London. Occupied in negotiations with Egyptian President Nasser and then with the Suez crisis, Whitehall did not press the matter. The issue continued to irritate the Pakistanis. At the beginning of

1957, Sir Bernard again urged Sultan Said to come to terms. The
sultan was not ready to give up Gawadur. Despite intensive
exploration, no large oil strike had yet been made in Oman. The
sultan claimed that it was important for him to hold onto territory
that might produce oil revenue. Pakistan repeated threats to
enforce an effective customs barrier. Convinced that too many
people, including high-ranking government officials in Karachi,
were involved in smuggling, and wanted no such barrier, Sultan
Said ignored these threats. If Pakistani troops moved into his
territory, he would call for international action. Burrows
attempted to persuade the sultan that in his dispute with Pakistan,
"with such a confused and uncertain history," he could not be
sure of international support. The sultan did not give in: "He
was all alone and he was being asked to make a decision which
would affect his whole country and all his people both now and
for generations to come."

Burrows suggested that Sultan Said balance two
possibilities. He might be criticized if he sold the territory, but
he also might be criticized if he did not sell and the Pakistanis
took action to turn Gawadur into a liability for Muscat. Prior to
using force, Pakistan would surely publish the generous offer it
made to purchase the territory. The sultan refused to move.
Burrows asked Consul General Chauncy to continue pressing.

The end of the rebellion in Nizwa led to the successful
extension of the sultan's influence into the interior, and at the
same time exploration for oil continued. It appeared to Burrows
that the sultan was pleased with his situation and the political
resident speculated that while the ruler of Muscat-Oman
remained truly loyal to his British connection, "I fear that he may
also realize that we have fewer friends than before in the Middle
East." Burrows continued to emphasize the advantage of selling
Gawadur, but he sympathized with the sultan's predicament:

> We are asking him to take a gamble with an
> important part of his patrimony in circumstances
> in which many of the determining factors are
> unknown, such as the presence of oil both in
> Muscat and in Gawadur, the future general
> policy of Pakistan and the administrative ability
> and will of the Pakistani authorities to impose
> control over the surrounding area in the face of
> serious personal and geographical obstacles.[45]

As Whitehall prepared for the June 1957 meeting of the
Baghdad Pact Council to be held in Karachi, the Foreign Office

briefed its delegation on Gawadur. The delegation was reminded that unlike other Persian Gulf rulers, the sultan was a sovereign ruler and not officially under British protection; nevertheless, he "leans heavily on our support." If the Pakistanis brought up the Gawadur question, the British delegates were to remind them that the Omani ruler had to be handled tactfully; to press him too hard might destroy the chance of reaching the desired agreement.[46]

Meanwhile, as a result of smuggling, trade in Gawadur increased, providing considerable revenue for the sultanate. The Foreign Office plotted strategy on 24 June. One suggestion was a Pakistani invitation to the sultan for a visit to Karachi, another a free zone within the port area at Gawadur.[47] During a visit to London by the Pakistani Prime Minister H.S. Suhrawardy at the end of June 1957, Sir Bernard and two Foreign Office officials met with him at the Claridges Hotel. Suhrawardy introduced a new factor; the Nawab of Makran also wanted Gawadur. The prime minister maintained that he would have to choose between sending the Pakistan army into Gawadur, or turning a blind eye while the Nawab of Makran sent in troops and made good his own claim to the territory. Sir Gilbert Laithwaite said that the Nawab had no claim to Gawadur. Suhrawardy disagreed. The Nawab's claim was first put forward in 1867."

Laithwaite responded that Britain recognized no other claim but the sultan's. Although H.M. Government wanted to cooperate with Pakistan and had attempted to convince the sultan to sell the territory, he had declined. Now, however, the Foreign Office would not oppose a customs cordon around Gawadur. When Laithwaite asked where the customs post would be set up, Suhrawardy was uncertain. Sir Bernard explained the sultan's dilemma. He had inherited Gawadur from his father. As an absolute ruler he had a unique responsibility to his people; he feared that if he gave up Gawadur, he would "lose face with his people; but if he were *compelled* to give it up, as a result of *force majeure,* this at any rate would not be the case."

Suhrawardy said he understood the sultan's problem, and was sympathetic. So if the Nawab of Makran used force, the problem would be resolved. Sultan Said would not lose face and Karachi would still pay for the territory if it was formally ceded. Sir Bernard saw flaws in the prime minister's reasoning. If the nawab, who was under Pakistani jurisdiction, invaded Gawadur, the sultan the much of the Arab world would certainly protest. But the prime minister persisted with the suggestion that if the nawab took the territory Britain could "turn a blind eye." The political resident demurred.[48]

The Gawadur issue was still unresolved when in July a new rebellion against the sultan in the interior of Oman required British intervention. There was considerable evidence that both Egypt and Saudi Arabia were assisting the rebels, and Britain wanted diplomatic cooperation from Pakistan. The Nasser government was using British activity in Oman "to whip up feeling against the United Kingdom." At the same time, London wished to avoid deterioration of relations with Saudi Arabia. The Baghdad Pact members, including Pakistan, had been involved in attempting "to draw King Saud away from his former close relations with the Egyptian government." Pakistan's Foreign Minister Firoz Khan Noon agreed that it was essential to move the Saudis away from Egypt, but he also warned that it would be impossible for Pakistan to support the sultan unless finally the Omani ruler agreed to relinquish Gawadur.[49] Successful British military action against the sultan's enemies gave the Pakistanis an opening to complain that it was time for the British to insist that Sultan Said make a deal on Gawadur.[50] Prime Minister Suhrawardy wrote a letter directly to Prime Minister Harold Macmillan at the end of August 1957; he referred to his keen disappointment that the sultan refused to yield, saying,

> When you have given such magnificent assistance to him, surely he would have listened to your advice had you made it plain to him that you were not prepared to alienate Pakistan for his sake, and that he must be reasonable and come to a settlement.[51]

Prime Minister Suhrawardy asked Macmillan once again to press the sultan during his scheduled October trip to London. Suhrawardy wrote, "I shall hold my soul in patience till then if I receive a word of encouragement from you."[52]

Prime Minister Macmillan responded to Suhrawardy, expressing pleasure that the Pakistani prime minister wrote directly to him. Macmillan said that Sir Bernard Burrows had done his best to persuade the sultan, but the Omani ruler said that he would respond in October or November during his trip to London. The British prime minister assured his Pakistani counterpart that he shared his disappointment. At this juncture, Macmillan advised that it would be unproductive to continue to press the sultan: "To do so might only risk causing him to make up his mind against making any move in the direction we both desire." The best course was to wait until his upcoming London

visit when Whitehall would strongly advise him to enter into
direct negotiations with Karachi. Macmillan concluded, "I fear
we must, as you say, possess our souls in patience."[53]
    Continuing the personal correspondence between the two
prime ministers Suhrawardy wrote to Macmillan on October 11,
declaring that India was taking advantage of the situation in
Gawadur to gain control of the province. He enclosed a
Pakistani intelligence report that supported his contention. Once
more the Pakistani leader insisted that the sultan had no right to
Gawadur and that he was "awaiting anxiously the results of the
forthcoming meeting between the sultan and yourself."[54] The
British high commissioner in Karachi was instructed to thank
Suhrawardy for his letter. The Foreign Office response
aggravated the political resident in Bahrain, who was upset by
the Pakistani intelligence report. According to Pakistani
intelligence, there was a slave market in Gawadur. Sir Bernard
claimed there was no slave market in the sultan's territory. When
attempts to bring slaves into Muscat were made, the sultan's
authorities took quick, effective action against the slave traders.
Likewise, the Pakistani contention that the sultan had large
business interests in India was false. The sultan had an Indian
connection only because his father lived in India and received a
small allowance from his son. Burrows considered the Pakistani
allegation that India offered to buy Gawadur to be absurd. Sir
Bernard wrote: "Surely it is unwise to let them think that we
believe all this nonsense?"[55] His question remained unanswered.
    The sultan, meanwhile, continued to postpone his trip to
London. The Pakistani president had hoped to meet with him
there in October. On a weekend visit to Lord Douglas Home's
house in Scotland, a British official asked the president if
perhaps he would be willing to meet the sultan in Bahrain on his
journey back to Pakistan. Disappointed that the sultan was not in
London, the president expressed little enthusiasm for a meeting
in Bahrain, but if the British considered the idea to be a good
one, he would agree. Before moving forward with the plan for a
Bahrain meeting, telegrams from Muscat indicated that the sultan
was not yet ready to resolve the situation. According to the
Pakistani president, "such a meeting might do more harm than
good."[56]
    Pakistani patience was not immediately rewarded. On 6
December, Lord Douglas Home told Pakistani Foreign Minister
Firoz Khan Noon that the sultan was unreasonable. He
continued to put off his proposed visit to London. Sir Firoz
declared that it would be wise for the Pakistanis to move against
the sultan in Gawadur, to send in Pakistani police to establish

customs posts, to occupy the airstrip, and to cancel the land grant given to the sultan's eighteenth-century ancestor. Noon, however, assured the foreign secretary that Pakistan would not act without British approval.[57] Confidentially, on his own initiative, the Pakistani high commissioner in London told the British Foreign Office that military action in Gawadur would be a mistake:

> It might give an excuse for India to take some action. Pakistan had secured very favorable international reactions over Kashmir because she had behaved well and India badly. Pakistan would lose all that advantage if she appeared to behave badly over Gawadur.[58]

He requested that Britain advise Pakistan against force. At the same time, he asked that the nature of his advice not be revealed to his own government. The Foreign Office agreed.[59]

Finally, in the spring of 1958 London resolved "to put the screws" on the sultan.[60] Among the arguments used to persuade him to give up Gawadur was that in order to develop the sultanate he needed foreign teachers and technicians. Clearly, he wanted to avoid admitting Egyptians, who might inspire leftist nationalism. If relations between Pakistan and Oman improved many Pakistanis could be hired.[61] Sultan Said suggested that the British would not react well if he asked for the return of the Kuria Muria Islands, which had been presented by the sultanate to Queen Victoria. Nevertheless, he finally capitulated in July 1958 not out of concern for Pakistan, but in order to help the British. Therefore, it was London's responsibility to arrange the terms of the agreement.[62] The sultan was an astute negotiator who could be counted on to read documents carefully and find any ambiguity that might work against him. The documents were prepared to his satisfaction. Prior to the transfer, Pakistan agreed to pay Oman £ 2,700,000 together with the equivalent of £ 300,000 in United States dollars. If oil was found in Gawadur, the sultanate would receive 10 percent of the profits for twenty-five years. Pakistan also agreed to remove all restrictions placed on the employment of Pakistani citizens serving in Muscat and to continue to supply both rice and technical assistance to the sultanate. In addition, residents of Gawadur who wished to remain subjects of the sultan were permitted to do so.[63]

Relinquishing Gawadur supplied the sultan with funds that could be used for development, providing some measure of relief from the primitive conditions that prevailed in the sultanate. The cautious Omani ruler, known as the "Scrooge of Arabia," remained unhappy about both spending money and introducing any sort of change. The sale of Gawadur provided satisfaction to the Pakistanis and relief to the British, but it did nothing at all for the sultan's long-suffering subjects. The decade of the 1950s ended with conditions in Muscat-Oman unchanged, little education, few roads, no economic opportunity.

NOTES

1. Letter, Hay to Bevin, Bahrain, 14 April 1948, FO 371/68317/XC 2312, Public Records Office, (hereafter cited as PRO).

2. Letter, Stewart to Hay, Muscat, 11 March 1948, FO 371/68317/XC 2312, PRO.

3. Letter, Hay to Bevin, Bahrain, 14 April 1948, FO 371/68317/XC 2312, PRO.

4. Letter, Ellison to Bevin, Muscat, 4 January 1949, FO 371/74958/XC1321, PRO.

5. Ibid.

6. Neil Innes, *Minister in Oman*, Cambridge: Oleander, 1987, p. 43.

7. Letter, Ellison to Bevin, Muscat, 4 January 1949, FO 371/74958/XC1321, PRO.

8. Innes, p. 43.

9. Report, Hay, Bahrain, 1948, FO 371/68319/XC 2329, PRO and Letter, Burrows to Galloway, London, 26 August 1948, FO 371/68318/XC 2329, PRO.

10. Letter, Hay to Bevin, Bahrain, 23 February 1949, FO 371/74957/XC 2329, PRO.

11. Note, London, April 30, 1949, PRO.

12. Minute, Burrows, London, April 1949, PRO.

13. The U.K. high commissioner in Pakistan was concerned that the sultan might travel on a Pakistani airline. Prior to the sultan's trip he wanted the ruler warned not to do so. He asked that the message be sent to Muscat in cypher. "You will appreciate my anxiety that my disparaging opinion should not, repeat, not be disclosed to Pakistani Government." Telegram 1552, U.K. Commissioner to Commonwealth Relations Office, Karachi, FO371/75041/1321, PRO.

14. Letter, Chauncy to Hay, 9 October 1950, PRO, and Hay to Secretary of State, Bahrain, 23 October 1950, FO 371/82077/XC 001605, PRO.

15. Note, Fry, London, 5 January 1955, FO 371/114642 XC001336, PRO.

16. Ibid., 21 January 1955, PRO.

17. Ibid., 22 February 1955, PRO.

18. Telegram 297, Commonwealth Relations Office to U.K. High Commissioner in Pakistan, London, 23 February 1955, PRO.

19. Letter, Chauncy to Burrows, Muscat, 13 February 1955, PRO.

20. Innes, p. 261.

21. Note, Kimber, 16 February 1955, FO 371/114642 XC001336, PRO.

22. Letter, James to Kimber, Karachi, 1 April 1955, PRO.

23. Telegram, U.K. High Commissioner to Commonwealth Relations Office, Karachi, 25 October 1949, FO 371/74957/xc 2329, PRO.

24. Note, Commonwealth Relations, London, November 1955, FO 371/114642 XC001336, PRO.

25. Ibid., Garner, 24 June 1955, PRO.

26. Minute, 7 July 1955, PRO.

27. Ibid., Samuel, 22 July 1955, PRO.

28. Ibid., 26 July 1955, PRO.

29. Ibid., Burrows, 27 July 1955, PRO.

30. Letter, Symon to Laithwaite, Karachi, 26 August 1955, PRO.

31. Ibid.

32. Dawn, 27 September 1955, PRO.

33. Note, J.G.L. London, 30 September 1955, PRO.

34. Ibid., Pickard, Ibid., 14 October 1955, PRO.

35. Extract from The Comment, Karachi, 23 October 1955, PRO.

36. Ibid, Commonwealth Relations, November 1955, PRO.

37. Telegram to Karachi, Bahrain, 24 November 1955, PRO.

38. Ibid., High Commissioner to Political Resident Persian Gulf, Karachi, 27 November 1955, PRO.

39. Ibid.

40. Telegram 865, Burrows to Foreign Office, Bahrain, 25 November 1955, PRO.

41. Telegram 908, Burrows to Foreign Office, Bahrain, 9 December 1955, PRO.

42. Ibid., 1765, High Commissioner to Foreign Office, Karachi, 14 December 1955, PRO.

43. Minute, Lord Home, London, 14 December 1955, PRO.

44. Ibid, Denson, London, 29 December 1955, PRO.

45. Telegram 1, Burrows to Foreign Office, 15 January 1957, Bahrain, FO 371/126928/XC001336, PRO.

46. Draft Brief For United Kingdom Delegation, London, June 1957, PRO.

47. Record of Meeting, London, 24 June 1957, PRO.

48. Note of a Meeting, London, 28 June 1957, PRO.

49. Telegram 1076, U.K. Commissioner to Commonwealth Relations Office, Karachi, 27 July 1957, PRO.

50. Telegram,1711, U.K. Commissioner to Bahrain, Karachi, 14 August 1957, PRO.

51. Letter, Suhrawardy to Macmillan, Karachi, 29 August 1957, FO 371/126929/XC001336, PRO.

52. Ibid.

53. Telegram 1887, Commonwealth Relations Office to High Commissioner in Pakistan, London, 7 September 1957, PRO.

54. Letter, Suhrawardy to Macmillan, Karachi, 11 October 1957, PRO.

55. Ibid, Burrows to Riches, Bahrain, 8 November 1957, PRO.

56. Minute, Gore, London, 4 November 1957, PRO.

57. Record of a conversation, London, 6 December 1957, PRO.

58. Ibid., 12 December 1957, Ibid.

59. Ibid.

60. Minute, London, 22 May 1958, FO 371/132791/EA 108427, PRO.

61. Record of a conversation, London, 4 June 1958, Fo 371/132791/EA 108427, PRO.

62. Minute, London, 10 July 1958, FO 371/13279/EA1084/44, PRO.

63. Minute, 26 July 1958, FO 371/132793/EA1084/59, PRO.

5

OIL

Although the sultanate remained poor; in the neighboring emirates, rich oil fields produced revenue used for development. Sultan Said was keenly interested in finding oil in the sultanate. With the provision that he exercised final authority, the sultan encouraged exploration in his domains. The possibility of rich deposits led to renewed American interest in Oman. From the decade of the 1920s British and American interests had competed for rights to Arab Gulf oil fields. One British offical declared in 1938 that "the competition for oil is not carried on philanthropic lines, and is at times over-exciting."[1] In the post-World War II era, this Anglo-American rivalry extended to Oman. Economic contention between British and American interests did not, however, interfere with political and military cooperation. London and Washington united in the desire to protect the gulf from both Nasserism and communist activity. At the same time, the United States recognized Britain's experience in the region and cooperated with the British effort to maintain the security of the gulf and the stability of Oman.

In April 1959, the United States Senate ratified a new treaty of Amity, Economic Relations and Consular Rights, Friendship and Commerce with the sultanate, a treaty that had been signed in Muscat on 20 December 1958. This treaty replaced the treaty of 1833 -- the last remaining treaty granting the United States extra-territorial rights. Washington had been eager to conclude a new agreement because of increasing interest in oil.

Negotiations with the sultan had been difficult. One of the first challenges faced by the Americans appointed to the negotiation team was how to reach the isolated sultanate without accepting a British invitation to travel on a Royal Air Force plane. In order to maintain American dignity, the State Department authorized the American negotiator, the consul general in Dhahran, Walter K. Schwinn, at last resort to charter a gulf aviation plane. Schwinn arrived in Muscat for his first visit with the sultan in June 1957. Like Consul John Ray, who served in Muscat forty-seven years earlier, the tall, blond American representative addressed the sultan as "Your Majesty." Minister of Foreign Affairs Neil McLeod Innes, did not object. He remarked that Americans liked to address the sultan as "Your Majesty." He did not discourage them because Sultan Said truly enjoyed hearing the title majesty and it appeared to be an appropriate recognition of his legal independence.[2] During his first meeting with Sultan Said, Schwinn gave the sultan a draft of the proposed treaty in both Arabic and English. After studying the documents, the sultan told Schwinn that lawyers had clearly prepared the treaty; the text was too long and too complicated. He wanted a shorter, simpler document. Schwinn reported to Washington that while the sultan had been educated in India and spoke excellent English, "Sultan's alert, bright eyes and easy delivery English mask medieval mentality and concepts." Schwinn cautioned that dealing with the sultan would take considerable time and patience.

Washington's goal was to protect the security of investments that Americans might make in Oman. The State Department wanted included in the treaty a binding assurance that disputes affecting investments would have a suitable forum for resolution. Hence, the State Department instructed Schwinn to include a provision in the proposed treaty that would mandate the referral of all disputes between the two parties to the International Court of Justice. Washington's proposal did not imply a desire to bring the sultanate before the court; the provision was merely to insure that in the event of possible misunderstandings, the parties would have the benefit of a recognized international forum.[3] As Schwinn had predicted negotiations moved slowly. American negotiators arrived in Muscat in February 1958 for a third round of talks. Schwinn was approached by a missionary serving in Muscat, Reverend Garett de Jong, who wanted information about how the proposed treaty would protect the right to proselytize. Schwinn explained that the 1833 treaty between Washington and Muscat had not provided for the right to proselytize. American missions in the sultanate operated solely on the basis of the ruler's goodwill and the United States would not ask a theocratic ruler, responsible for the orthodoxy of his people, to sanction proselytization. The new treaty included a provision promising freedom of religion, the right to worship, to hold any sort of religious belief, but did not guarantee the right to conduct missionary activities. As a result, after the signing of the treaty, American missionaries active in the sultan's territory would continue to depend on his goodwill alone.

The sultan continued to refuse Washington's request that disputes be referred to the International Court. His existing treaties with Britain and India did not contain such a provision. According to Schwinn, the sultan did not truly understand how the court functioned and hesitated to permit any third party to interfere in a treaty between the two nations. The sultan announced that he did not need a new treaty, that he would be satisfied simply to abrogate the archaic treaty of 1833. Hence, Washington was faced with accepting a treaty without a provision to refer disputes to the International Court or no treaty at all. At this juncture, the State Department considered the prospect of rich oil resources in the sultanate. American business wanted access and a treaty was necessary to secure American economic interests. The State Department capitulated. Washington withdrew its demand for inclusion in the treaty of a provision to refer disputes to the International Court.[4] But it was not until 1972 that the United States established an embassy in the sultanate. The first American to serve, Ambassador William Stoltzfus, Jr., was also accredited to Kuwait and resided there. It was only in 1974, fifty nine years after Sultan Taimour expressed regret at Washington's decision to close the American consulate in Muscat that the United States sent a resident ambassador to Muscat, Ambassador William Wolle, who arrived in the sultanate a year after Sayyid Faisal bin Ali opened the Omani embassy in Washington.[5]

Following President Dwight D. Eisenhower's request that Congress ratify the new treaty with Muscat, Oman, and Dependencies, from Damascus a representative of the exiled government of the imamate protested, accusing the Americans of interference in Oman. The Saudi Arabian government also protested the treaty because the terms recognized the rights of the sultan outside Muscat. Washington informed Jidda that in the nineteenth century the term "Muscat" and the term "Oman" were often used interchangeably and from the beginning of the twentieth century the term "Muscat and Oman" was used to designate the sultan's realm. Washington had no intention of

discussing with the Saudis how another ruler referred to his
territories. At the same time, the State Department assured Jidda
that the only purpose of the treaty was to regularize commercial
relations between the United States and the sultanate. Saudi
Prince Faisal was not pleased. He proclaimed that he would
continue to assist the exiled Omanis against the sultan.[6]

Although the rebellion in the interior had been crushed,
Saudi Arabia, Egypt, and other Arab states continued to support
the imamate in exile and, in 1961, the issue was again before the
United Nations. British support for the sultan was characterized
as a continuation of imperialism. When the sultan invited retired
British Consul Leslie Chauncy to return to Muscat to serve as his
personal adviser, the Foreign Office feared the possibility of
negative publicity. The Arabian Department told its United
Nations mission in New York that in the event members of
friendly delegations questioned Chauncy's appointment, officials
were to respond that the sultan made the appointment entirely on
his own initiative, without prior consultation with Britain.
Chauncy had, however, consulted the Foreign Office before
accepting the sultan's invitation. Clearly, if the Foreign Office
had advised Chauncy that acceptance was prejudicial to British
interests, he would have declined. Although there were political
disadvantages connected with the former consul's return to
Oman, the Arabian Department concluded that the advantages
outweighed the disadvantages. Chauncy's position was unique
and perhaps he would be able to institute necessary reforms.[7] In
April, it appeared initially that the State Department might not
support the sultan in the United Nations. Reluctantly, however,
Washington agreed to do so. The new American assistant
secretary for Near Eastern and South Asian affairs, Phillip
Talbot, authorized State Department representative Hermann
Eilts to discuss with the British the possibility that more could be
done to convince the sultan to play an active role in the defense
of his interests, both domestically and internationally. Eilts
suggested that when Sultan Said next visited London an
American Embassy official speak to him and propose that he
spend more time in Muscat or appoint someone with authority to
represent him there. The British had already offered the sultan
the same advice[8]

In May, officials at the British Embassy in Washington
expressed gratitude to the State Department for American
assistance at the United Nations. A British official took up the
earlier American suggestion that when the sultan next visited
London a member of the American Embassy speak to him there.
Eilts now had reservations. He said that "the risk of giving

offense outweighed the possible advantage to be gained." But the retiring consul general from Dhahran, Schwinn, who was present at the meeting, expressed the view that an American conversation with the sultan most likely would do no good, but neither would it do any harm.[9]   In a subsequent conversation, Eilts said that since the sultan did nothing to help himself, it was very difficult for Washington to support him. Nevertheless, the United States was considering taking some sort of initiative with the sultan, . Although the State Department had no illusions that Washington would succeed where London had failed; at least it was worth trying.[10]

After the rebellion on the Jebel Akhdar, no progress had been made. Health care remained primitive. Patients from the interior traveled for days to reach the mission hospital in Mutrah. Space was so scarce that often two patients shared one bed. Family members stayed to assist the sick, cooking meals and tending their children in the hospital rooms. Goats wandered through the corridors. Education too remained primitive. There were only three schools in the sultanate in 1961, Standards were low. Eighty percent of the 270 boys attending the Mutrah school in 1961 were Khoja and Baluch boys, sons of local merchants. Although many shaikhs and walis in the interior appealed to the sultan for the opportunity to educate their sons, the sultan still insisted that education would introduce dangerous new ideas. Hence, he opposed opening any sort of school in the interior. As a result, the Omanis who had the means sent their sons to boarding schools in Bahrain, Kuwait, and Qatar. These boys were exposed to a wide variety of ideas, including communism. They were also introduced to Arab nationalism and the rhetoric of Egyptian President Gamal Abdul Nasser. The sultan's refusal to educate boys at home where they could be "properly indoctrinated" with loyalty to the ruler and to their own country resulted in the exposure of young Omanis to exactly the sort of education the sultan most feared. The British continued to urge Sultan Said to provide education, especially a boarding school for the sons of tribal leaders. Such a school would keep young men from good families in the country and provide the sultanate with educated men so that it would no longer be necessary to hire foreigners for all technical jobs, positions in agriculture , and medicine.

In December 1962, Arab countries supporting the exiled imamate brought the subject before the United Nations once again calling on the world body to recognize the independence of the people of Oman and demanding the withdrawal of foreign troops. The resolution put forward by the sultan's opponents failed to gain the required two-thirds majority. The resolution was unsuccessful as a result of intensive British lobbying in New York. Defending the sultan was increasingly more difficult because of the propaganda campaign of the sultan's opposition, but also because of criticism from British allies, who questioned British support for Muscat. Since the sultan refused to allow reporters into his country, it appeared that he probably had something to hide.

At the beginning of 1962, British Secretary of State for War John Profumo planned to visit Muscat. The Foreign Office prepared a brief for Profumo, suggesting that he emphasize the danger that supporters of the imamate would likely renew their efforts at the United Nations. The sultan should be prepared to counter the attack. Profumo could suggest that the sultan would benefit if he sent a personal representative abroad to speak on his behalf, and if he joined some international organizations. He might consider the World Health Organization and the Food and Agricultural Organization. Such action would enhance the sultanate's prestige as well as secure technical assistance from experts. Visiting London the previous September, Sultan Said told reporters that he was considering membership in the two international organizations. Earlier the sultan had also remarked that if London agreed to pay the annual subscription, which was too expensive for him, he would join the World Health Organization. Profumo was advised to suggest that the required sum was reasonable and within the sultan's means. Finally, Profumo might express his satisfaction at the very successful development of the Sultan's Armed Forces, SAF. Nevertheless, here too there was a serious problem. Most SAF officers were foreigners. The sultan had no alternative but to rely on foreign officers. Yet, the presence of these officers handicapped British efforts to refute charges of colonialism and accusations that the sultanate was not truly an independent state. Profumo could tell the sultan that the British were ready and willing to train suitably qualified Muscatis to replace the foreign officers.[11]

Meanwhile, prior to the arrival of Secretary Profumo, Political Resident William Luce wrote a confidential letter to Sir Roger Stevens at the Foreign Office. The sultan had expressed animosity toward the secretary of state for war. The sultan considered Profumo to be a leader of a sizable Whitehall faction opposed to the continuation of support for the sultanate. Sultan Said did not provide evidence to support his prejudice against Profumo, but he held fast to that prejudice. Hence, it was unlikely that Profumo would have any influence at all during his visit to Muscat.[12] Nevertheless, the sultan finally agreed to apply for membership in the World Health Organization. When the World Health Assembly considered the sultanate's application in May 1962 a coalition of Muslim and communist states -- Iraq, Mali, Sudan, Yugoslavia, the Soviet Union, Saudi Arabia, and the United Arab Republic -- spoke out against it. The attack on the sultan was so violent that the Irish chairman was unable to restore order. The delegate from Ceylon suggested that the item be deferred. Fearing the likelihood that the application would be voted down, the British delegate agreed.[13]

Sayyid Tariq too was unable to influence the sultan. He was unhappy in Muscat, distressed by the absence of substantial development and the lack of educational opportunities in the sultanate. During the decade of the 1950s, he had played a role in the government, often representing his brother on ceremonial occasions. He wished to assume serious responsibility. Although the sultan gave him the title Inspector of Walis, Sultan Said denied his half-brother the opportunity to do anything substantial. Without real employment, Tariq played bridge and went hunting.[14] The sultan's younger brother grew increasingly concerned about the future of the sultanate and about the destiny of his own sons. Unable to effect change in Muscat, Tariq left the sultanate with his family in 1963. He wanted his children to be educated and hoped that in the future they would be able to return to their country prepared to play an important role in its administration.[15]

Further adding to the British burden, capital punishment in the sultanate became an issue for London in the decade of the 1960s. In February 1961, Sultan Said instructed Patrick Waterfield, who had returned to Muscat under contract to the ruler, to arrange with the minister of interior for the trial by Sharia Court of four alleged murderers incarcerated in Fort Jalali. In the event the court found any of the accused guilty and ordered the death penalty, it would be the responsibility of the Sultan's Armed Forces to organize a firing squad, commanded by a non-British officer. Those sentenced to death would be executed "in the traditional manner," in public, at the bottom of the steps leading from the jetty to Fort Mirani. British officials were concerned that a public execution would trouble the western democracies and "offer a gift" to the sultan's enemies,"who will regardless of the facts, call the executions political." British officials considered how to react to the possible executions. The British declared that they had no desire to interfere in the sultanate's penal processes but wanted the sultan to realize that if civilians were to be executed, it might be best for the police to carry out the execution and to do it in the interior of the country, "or anywhere but on the Sultan's front door-step."[16]

Since the SAF was mainly British, London did not approve the use of that force for an execution. It had been years since a criminal was executed in Oman, and the renewal of executions might nullify the sultan's recent release of some former rebels from prison. The Foreign Office feared that any execution would be a "stab in the back" for British efforts to defend Muscat at the United Nations.[17] Consul General John Phillips reminded the sultan that when the previous September he had assumed his post, the ruler requested that he always speak frankly. At the risk of being told to mind his own business, Phillips presented the British reaction to a possible execution, including the caveat that the effect of a photograph in the world press would be unhappy. The timing of any execution would increase London's difficulties at the United Nations when the General Assembly reconvened. Phillips praised the past administration of justice in the sultanate in a condescending manner, saying that compared to the other states in the region, Omani penal processes were humane and reasonable. The British Consul appealed to Sultan Said to consider exercising clemency, or at least executing the condemned out of the public view.[18]

Although the sultan admitted that he had asked Phillips always to be frank with him, now that he had, the ruler was offended. Sultan Said was ruler of a Muslim country that followed the Sharia Law. He had discussed the possibility of executions with Brigadier Waterfield and had explained the traditional manner of carrying out executions. However, he had not authorized Waterfield to discuss the matter. He expected obedience. In the event he gave an order that conflicted with an officer's duty to the queen, the officer could resign. He would not have the character of his army conform to English standards. Waterfield acknowledged that he had not been authorized by the sultan to discuss a possible execution. He agreed to apologize, explaining that he was concerned about the negative effect the proposed firing squad would have on SAF morale. A British officer, Lt. Colonel Read, had already informed Colonel David Smiley that he would not carry out such an order.[19]

Despite the best efforts of British officials to prevent a public execution in Muscat, on 16 September, below Fort Mirani an Omani SAF soldier, who eight months before had killed a civilian, was executed. This was the first execution in Muscat since 1938. Contrary to custom, the victim's relatives refused to accept blood money. The sentence was carried out by the victim's family. SAF troops escorted the prisoner from jail and kept back the assembled crowd. With the exception of Brig. Waterfield, no British officers were present.[20] The prisoner was not blindfolded, nor was he tied to a plank. Initially the fifteen-year-old son of the murdered man attempted to execute the condemned man using an eighteenth-century rifle that misfired three times. The boy handed the rifle to an older relative, who borrowed a .303 rifle from an SAF guard. The first shot hit the prisoner's chest; the second, fired five minutes later, hit his forehead.[21]

London discussed the possible ramifications of the execution. The Foreign Office considered it likely that when news of the execution gained international attention, Britain would be criticized for supporting the sultan. Parliament, which supported the sultanate with the taxpayers' money, would express outrage at the possibility that in the future a British subject might be executed in the sultanate. Robert Walmsley suggested that readiness to commute a death sentence in exchange for blood money "is more liberal than orthodox Western attitudes" Nevertheless, he agreed that Britons should not be exposed to the sultan's system of justice. Sir John Wyatt did not consider the Muslim system to be liberal. "The concept of murder as a private wrong and, therefore, as a subject for private vengeance is repugnant to the tenets of Western Humanism and Christian ethics."[22]

Defending the execution, the sultan explained that he had confirmed the sentence of a man who was guilty of murder and that shooting was the means of execution in the sultanate. Unlike the Saudis, the Omanis did not behead the condemned. Finally, the procedure was perfectly proper under Sharia law.[23] The sultan's explanation only confirmed Sir John Wyatt's prejudice that the Omani ruler did not administer justice. Some Foreign Office officials wanted to warn the sultan that to insure British support, he would have to leave criminal jurisdiction over British subjects to Her Majesty's Government. Other officials expressed concern that such a threat might offend Sultan Said, who well understood that strategically and politically support for the sultanate was in British interest.[24]

Political Resident Luce visited the sultan in Salalah at the end of October. When Luce broached the subject of public executions, the sultan remained calm. He, of course, did not attach importance to public opinion, but understood that the British government had to take it into account. The sultann agreed to ask the qadis if the Sharia law required execution to take place in the capital city. If not, in the future he would order executions to be carried out in the location where the crimes were committed. On the question of who was to carry out an execution, the sultan did not move from his opinion that executions had to be carried out by a relative of the victim. It was a cardinal point of the sultan's policy "not to expose himself to any accusations by the bigoted Ibadhis that he is departing from the strict letter of the Sharia law." Luce suggested, however, that it might be possible to insure that the executioner, whoever he was, received training in the use of a rifle, and that the rifle used be reliable.

Although Britain wanted to avoid public executions in Muscat, Luce pointed out that London was not in a position to pressure the sultan. In 1961, Britain was engaged in protecting neighboring Kuwait from the threat of invasion by Iraq, and military facilities in Muscat were essential.[25] By the end of the year, London was satisfied that the issue of capital punishment in the sultanate would not become an embarrassment for H.M. Government. The sultan confided to his adviser Leslie Chauncy that he was "thoroughly dissatisfied" with how the September execution had been carried out. He also agreed that in the future no British subject would have any involvement at all in executions, and that executioners would be trained to do their job.[26]

Hugh Boustead, who for three years had toured the interior of Oman and the Batinah in his capacity as development secretary, witnessed the execution from his verandah. From that vantage point he described to his colleagues how one of the sultan's relatives filmed the scene.[27] Boustead pleaded for change:

> Surely, at the present time with H.M.G. in support of the Ruler, holding him in the saddle by military force and enabling his writ to run throughout Oman, while civilization closes in on Oman, and when more and more young men return from Kuwait and Bahrain to visit their country, there will be an outcry against this which will react very sorely for the Ruler. How will H.M.G. stand before the world?[28]

An experienced administrator with years of service in the Middle East, Boustead attempted to set up health centers, develop agriculture, and plan roads. He later called his three years in Oman "intensely frustrating."[29]

The sultan consulted the qadis, who confirmed that executions had to be held in Muscat. The major reason for such executions was to deter crime. The more public the scene, the greater the deterrent. Hence, executions would be carried out in the traditional spot. The sultan, however, wanted to avoid future executions and would encourage every effort to press relatives to accept blood money.[30] One British official commented that London should remember that until the middle of the nineteenth century public executions took place in Britain.[31]

Sir John Wyatt continued to express concern about possible future executions in Muscat and wanted to engage in additional discussion with the sultan. Wyatt did not advocate the abolition of capital punishment, but a change in procedure. In Qatar, public executions were carried out at dawn by the police. Wyatt advised the sultan to follow the Qatar plan. He also expressed concern about the possibility that in the future a Christian might be placed before a firing squad. "If this should happen, heads will roll in Whitehall as well as Muscat."[32]

Despite Foreign Office fears, although rare, traditional executions continued. The following November a slave of the Beni Shikail, who had killed two men and wounded a third, was executed. According to the Sharia law, in the case of a double murder without motive or defense, neither blood money nor imprisonment was an option; execution was mandatory. The execution was carried out by a relative of one of the victims; with one round from a .303 rifle he hit a target that had been placed on the back of the condemned man. Colonel Waterfield had advance knowledge of the planned execution but had been forbidden by the sultan to report to London before the execution took place. Waterfield assured the Foreign Office that the execution had been properly carried out and that other than himself no British subject had been present. At least one thousand people attended the execution, including children. All behaved with dignity. The execution took place while the United Nations was in the midst of debate on Oman. Whitehall once more expressed fear that if such news reached the press, it would injure the sultanate.[33]

The Foreign Office was also concerned with the question of slavery in the sultanate. Most Arab Gulf rulers had banned slavery after World War II and the ban had been effective. There was no open trade and no established routes. Yet, domestic slavery continued and was accepted as a normal feature of social life. In Muscat most domestic slaves were the children of slaves who had been born into their master's household. The sultan scrupulously observed his obligation to cooperate fully in the suppression of the slave trade and consistently approved all slave applications for manumission.[34] The *Sunday Pictorial* of 23 June 1961 published an article that brought the slavery question to the attention of the British public. Consul General Phillips explained to London that slaves could obtain manumission by applying at his office. The consulate had processed an average of eighteen applications yearly since 1951. True, some slaves were badly treated. On the other hand, there were some cases of manumitted slaves, "having tasted the responsibilities of freedom, who happily returned to their former masters." Phillips reported that since the ouster of the Saudis from Buraimi, traffic in slaves had been rare.[35]

Meanwhile, the search for oil intensified and the companies involved faced numerous problems, including climate, accessibility, and security. The sultan closely followed the activities of those he permitted to enter his country. Because prospects looked good for the discovery of a rich field with a direct outlet to the Indian Ocean, in 1953 he had agreed to accept financial assistance from International Petroleum Company (IPC) to pay a police force to protect oil workers and equipment in Huqf. Recruiting the men was not an easy task. The British recommended that in order to provide a well-trained force around which to build a local Omani force, one hundred men from the Aden Levies -- Arabs who served under British officers -- be detached for temporary service under the sultan. The sultan consented.[36]

Occasionally there was discord between the sultan and oil company representatives. In 1956, Petroleum Development Oman appointed Sir William O'Brien Lindsay as its chief local representative. Sir William and the sultan had several disagreements. In February 1958, Sir William told the Omani ruler that it appeared that he did not like to deal with senior officials and wanted only to deal with juniors. The sultan insisted that Lindsay leave the sultanate. Sir William quickly resigned.[37]

In 1959, still searching for a large strike of good quality oil, IPC moved its main rig and camp to Haima, approximately one hundred miles inland northwest from the company base at Duqqam, on the Arabian Sea. A British visitor called the spot one of the most desolate he had ever seen. The Europeans employed at the camp were expected to remain for a year before receiving leave.[38] Local labor too worked in Haima, the Harisis, a nomadic people without a recognized shaikh. These workers received free food and housing and were paid between three and four rupees, a day, good wages in the sultanate.[39] The British encouraged the sultan to permit employment of Omanis. Sultan Said resisted. When Adenese working for Cities Services in Dhofar went on strike, Chauncy asked the sultan why the company did not employ Dhofaris. The sultan replied that because the company employed outsiders, who were more sophisticated than the locals, the company had to provide better working conditions. Meanwhile, Omanis worked abroad acquiring new skills that in the future would be useful at home.[40] By the end of 1959 some oil interests drilling in Oman were discouraged. Exploration was extremely expensive and although there was evidence of oil, as yet no substantial strike had occurred. However, hopes of finding oil were raised when, in 1961, Petroleum Development Oman and City Services revived drilling operations. Finally, oil in commercial quantities was discovered in 1964. Three years later, after the construction of a long pipeline from Fahud -- the largest field -- to the export terminal near Muscat at Mina Al Fahal, production began. [41]

Despite the oil strikes, unrest continued in the sultanate. Rebel activity to topple the sultan was sometimes reduced, but never completely extinguished. Violence was an ever-present concern. Two fatal mine incidents took place in February 1961, a Landrover explosion near Rustaq killed a British solider, and a taxi carrying passengers, including several women and children, exploded near Muscat killing three people.[42] Three months later, a Muscat mailbag exploded in Bahrain a few hours prior to loading. As a result, passengers departing from Bait-al-Falaj were searched and afterwards were segregated from others. Baggage too was, of course, inspected.[43] In December, the sultan's half-brother, the wali of Sur, Sayyid Majid survived an explosion caused by mines in a box placed against the outside wall of his fort tower. In this incidence it was unclear whether or not the explosives were placed by rebels or unsuccessful litigants in a land dispute.[44] The insurgents also worked outside the sultanate, attempting to sabotage merchant shipping and communications in the gulf. Following an explosion attributed to the dissidents, the *M.V. Dara* sank off the coast of Dubai on 17 April 1961, killing 236 passengers and crew members.

During the first eight months of 1962, there were sixteen mining incidents and twelve sniping incidents, which produced twenty-four casualties. The rebels most often hit civilians, resulting in a general loss of sympathy for their movement. Rebel leaders, who since 1954 had attempted to join the Arab League, were again rebuffed in 1962, and this blow to the movement appeared to create a degree of disillusionment among both leaders and followers.[45]

In the 1960s, the British government vigorously pursued the objective of building the Omani military to insure that the sultanate would be able to defend itself without open British intervention. In order to achieve the desired result, the Foreign Office wanted evidence of progress toward a viable state with an indigenous civil and military administration, which would enable Muscat to conduct its own domestic and foreign affairs.[46] Reform of the sultan's administration appeared to be essential. The sultan had traveled several times to London, but at the end of 1961 he had not visited his capital in four years. He remained in Salalah, separated from the majority of his subjects by 500 miles of desert. The conduct of one member of the royal family, governor of Muscat, Sayyid Shihab, underlined the capricious nature of the establishment. An elderly lady obtained permission to build a small home on a certain site; after the building was completed, Sayyid Shihab, saw the structure and was displeased. He ordered the woman to move the house within four hours. On another occasion Sayyid Shihab was erroneously told that the leader of the Hawasinah tribesmen guarding the Bab al Matha'ib gate, a gate reserved for military traffic, had allowed a civilian car to enter. Shihab fired the tribesman and ordered him to leave Muscat by sunset. "Being sensible as well as terrified, the gate keeper did so without a word." Shihab also refused to make most Omani passports valid for the Hajj without payment of a substantial deposit. He referred to the payment as a deposit, but the conditions for retrieving the money made it almost impossible for most to get it back.[47] Upon return from the Hajj, Shihab demanded that pilgrims wishing a refund show evidence of a Saudi immigration stamp on their passports. Most pilgrims, however, were sent from Bahrain to Dammam by agents who passed them through the ports using comprehensive lists, rather than passports. Thus, they did not have a Saudi stamp. Shihab claimed that his intention was to prevent dissatisfied subjects from using the pilgrimage as a cover to leave the country to find work abroad, or worse, to join the rebels.[48]

Support for the immamate remained a concern. Without recognizing the right of the United Nations to discuss the internal affairs of the sultanate, Sultan Said invited a United Nations representative to visit him in 1963. The Secretary General appointed the Swedish ambassador to Spain, Herbert de Ribbing as his personal representative. At the end of May, Ambassador de Ribbing met with the sultan in Salalah and later with Imam Ghalib bin Ali in Saudi Arabia. Nothing was resolved and the United Nations continued to discuss the issue. The sultan sent a cable to New York, noting that the question of Oman was again on the agenda, now "even more incongruously" in the committee that dealt with trusteeship matters and non-self-governing territories. Sultan Said announced that his territories were sovereign and independent, that he alone was responsible for their government. Nevertheless, while on a visit to London in September he once again agreed to meet with a United Nations representative. The sultan stated that no leader of a Middle Eastern country would permit the United Nations to interfere in relations between a ruler and his subjects. The sultanate was governed according to customs that had developed over a long period. Outsiders did not understand the Omani system and attempted to discuss the affairs of the sultanate in modern terms, which did not apply to local conditions. The problems in his domains had been created by outsiders, who had seized upon a rebellion by a few self-interested tribal shaikhs. These outsiders had no genuine interest in the welfare of his people. [49]

Meanwhile, anticipating that oil would bring wealth to the sultanate, in the summer of 1963 a British official expressed concern about the future of the sultan's twenty-three-year-old son Sayyid Qaboos who, after completing his education in England, would shortly return to the sultanate. Although, as a young man Sultan Said had assumed absolute power, he appeared to consider his son a child who required a long period at Salalah, "among his elders and betters." [50] Sayyid Qaboos had, however, graduated from Sandhurst, completed a six-month attachment to the 11th Brigade at Minden, and gone on a world tour. In the summer of 1963, the prince was in England visiting centers of industry and public administration. Keenly interested in the sultan's successor, the Foreign Office took every opportunity to insure that he became familiar with "the British way of doing things" London viewed the sultan as a firm friend and wanted Sayyid Qaboos to have the same commitment to Britain after he succeeded his father. [51] The Foreign Office was also concerned about preparing the young prince to deal with the responsibility of the wealth that appeared certain:

> He is about to enter into his Kingdom with the likelihood of possessing one vital and dangerous power which his father has never had: wealth from oil. There will be changes. My concern is that the Sultan will not give him enough responsibility to get dug in before the wind blows. In my judgment it is about to blow soon. [52]

The sultan, however, did not recognize the importance of permitting his son to play a role in the government. Sayyid Qaboos had never seen Muscat or any of his father's territories outside of Dhofar, and upon his return from England was not permitted to do so. He was confined to Salalah with no responsibility.[53]

Little changed in the sultanate; the sultan continued to impede development and refused to spend the money provided by the oil wealth of his domains. Then, unwilling to continue carrying the economic burden of securing the Arab Gulf, the British Labour government ignored the ghost of Lord Curzon and announced in February 1966 a major change in defense policy, a sharp reduction in the British military commitment outside of Europe. Britain prepared to withdraw from Aden by the end of 1968. Prior to the British announcement, the Egyptian president had reached an agreement with Saudi Arabia to withdraw from North Yemen, but then Nasser declared that he had changed his view and would maintain Egyptian troops in Yemen to liberate South Arabia.[54] Despite earlier conflicts with the British and a record of cooperation with the Egyptians, Saudi King Faisal was sufficiently concerned by Nasserite activities in the region to request in May 1967 that London reconsider its decision to leave Aden.[55] London refused. When the British abandoned Aden at the end of 1967, a year before the originally announced deadline, left-wing extremists assumed power and established the People's Democratic Republic of Yemen.

The British proceeded with plans to leave the Arab Gulf. At a cabinet meeting in January 1968, the government decided to complete the withdrawal from east of the Suez in March 1971. Fearing radical Arab nationalism, the sultan's neighbors were distressed by the British announcement. In order to convince the British to remain, the rulers of Dhabi, Abu Dhabi, Bahrain, and Qatar offered to assist with the cost of maintaining a British military presence.[56] London refused to reconsider and moved forward with plans for withdrawal.

As a result of the British decision, the United States was concerned that the Soviet Union might attempt to secure bases in the region, bases that would threaten Washington's relations with the Saudis and Iranians. Embroiled in Vietnam, Washington was unwilling to assume the traditional British role in the Gulf. In 1969, President Richard Nixon announced the Nixon Doctrine, which called on Asian nations, insofar as they were able, to handle their own defense. The State Department considered Iran the suitable candidate to fill what had been a traditional British responsibility. As a result, Washington provided Iran with advanced military equipment and Iran became "America's surrogate as guardian of peace and stability in the Gulf."[57]

Prior to relinquishing their traditional role in the Arab Gulf, the British performed an important service for Muscat-Oman. With British cooperation Sayyid Qaboos bin Said, still confined to Dhofar, deposed his father in July 1970. An American archaeologist, Wendell Phillips, who was befriended by Sultan Said, recounted that before the discovery of oil in commercial quantities, during long treks through the desert the sultan exclaimed: "Just think what I can do for my people when we have oil."[58] But when oil produced income, the sultan did nothing. His people continued to live without medical care, education, or opportunity. Thus, while in future years oil revenue would contribute to the development of the sultanate, discovery of oil did not free the Omani people. The sultan's subjects were liberated by the coup d'état led by Sayyid Qaboos, the coup that forced Sultan Said to abdicate and retire to London.

NOTES

1. Quoted in Records of the *Royal Central Asia Society*, 6 April 1938, p. 356.

2. Neil Innes, *Minister in Oman,* Cambridge: Oleander, 1987, p. 238.

3. Miriam Joyce, "Washington and Treaty-Making with the Sultan of Muscat and Oman," in *Middle Eastern Studies*, January 1994, pp. 145-147.

4. Ibid., pp. 148-149.

5. Hermann Eilts, *A Friendship Two Centuries Old: The United States and the Sultanate of Oman,* Washington: The Middle East Institute, 1990, p. 18.

6. Joyce, p. 152.

7. Letter, Arabian Department to Chancery, London, 11 April 1961, FO 371/156816/XC/164520, Public Records Office (hereafter cited as PRO.

8. Letter, Weir to Walmsley, Washington, 26 April 1961, FO 371/156773 XC 164523, PRO.

9. Letter, Weir to Jones, Washington, 17 May 1961, FO 371/156773/XC164523, PRO.

10. Letter, Speares to Jones, Washington, 23 June 1961, FO 371/156773/XC 164523, PRO.

11. Brief for the Secretary of State for War: Points for Discussion with the Sultan of Muscat and Oman, London, December 1962, FO 371/162550/XC2122, PRO.

12. Letter, Luce to Stevens, Bahrain, 6 January 1962, FO 371/162850/XC 2122, PRO.

13. Letter, Black to Wyatt, London, 31 October 1962, FO 371/162853/XC 002136, PRO.

14. Report, Muscat, 1961, FO 371/156758/XC164523, PRO.

15. Letter, Luce to Walmsley, Bahrain, 19 December 1962, FO 371/168721, PRO.

16. Letter, Phillips to Man, Muscat, 5 February 1961, FO 371/156815/XC 164523, PRO.

17. Letter, Beaumont to Phillips, London, 21 February1961, PRO.

18. Letter, Phillips to Sultan Taimour, Muscat, 6 March 1961, PRO.

19. Letter, Phillips to Mann, Muscat, 8 April 1961, PRO.

20. Telegram 118, Pridham to Foreign Office, Muscat, 16 September 1961, PRO.

21. Letter, Cooper to Consul-General, Muscat, 17 September 1961, PRO.

22. Minute, Jones, 21 September 1961, PRO.

23. Ibid.

24. Minutes, September-October 1962, London, PRO.

25. Letter, Luce to Walmsley, Bahrain, 4 November 1961, PRO.

26. Letter, Phillips to Man, Muscat, 28 December 1961, PRO.

27. Minute, London, 5 April 1962. FO 371/162876/1618, PRO.

28. Note, Boustead, Muscat, 18 October 1961, FO 371/156818/XC 164523, PRO.

29. Hugh Boustead, *The Wind of Morning*, London: Chatto & Windus, 1971, p. 219.

30. Letter, Phillips to Man, Muscat, 15 March 1962, FO 371/162876/1618, PRO.

31. Minute, London, 28 March 1962, FO 371/162876/1618, PRO.

32. Minute, London, 5 April 1962, FO 371/162876/1618, PRO.

33. Letter, Greaves to Brown, Muscat, 26 November 1962, FO 371/ 162876/1618, PRO.

34. Letter, Middleton to Lloyd, Bahrain, 23 May1959, FO 371/1403051/BA2184/1, PRO.

35. Letter, Phillips to Wyatt, Muscat, 11 July 1961, FO 371/136716/XC 1618, PRO. The political resident in Muscat noted in 1950 that Saudi slave traders arrived in Buraimi in November with a

caravan of about fifty slaves; some perhaps from Oman. Note, Hay, 29 March 1950, FO 371/82123/XC 001605, PRO.

36. Minute, 23 January 1953, FO 371/104357/EA120/13, PRO.

37. Telegram 218, Burrows to Foreign Office, Bahrain, 21 February 1958, FO 371/132848/EA/1530/8, PRO. According to Chauncy, "The Sultan's character is such that no one but the person himself can do anything to put the Sultan off him."

38. Minute, London, 4 February 1959, FO 371/140229/BA1535/3, PRO.

39. Minute, Middleton, FO 371/140229/BA1535/1, PRO.

40. Letter, Chauncy to Given, Muscat, 10 February 1958, FO 371/132848/ EA/536/6, PRO.

41. *Oman '93,* Ministry of Information, Muscat, p. 90.

42. Annex to Monthly Diary, Muscat, February 1961, FO 371/156759/XC/164523, PRO.

43. Annex to Monthly Diary, Muscat, May 1961, FO 371/156759/XC/164523, PRO.

44. Administration Report, Muscat, 1961, FO 371/156758/XC 164523, PRO.

45. Telegram 53, Review of Omani Rebel Activity, London. FO 371/162853/XC002136, PRO.

46. Letter, Walmsley to Luce, London, 12 March 1962, FO 371/156758/XC/164523, PRO.

47. Annex to Monthly Diary, Muscat, June 1961, FO371/156759/XC/164523, PRO.

48. Letter, Consulate to Residency, Muscat, 22 May 1961, FO371/156816/XC/164520, Ibid.

49. Oman: Report of Ad Hoc Committee in *UN Monthly Chronicle,* New York: Office of Public Information, March 1965, pp. 29-30.

50. Letter, Duncan to Black, Muscat, 6 August 1963, FO 371/168725/XC7611, PRO.

51. Minute, Black, London, 26 April 1963, FO 371/168725/XC7611, PRO.

52. Letter, Duncan to Black, Muscat, 6 August 1963, FO 371/168725/XC7611, PRO; Minute, Black, London, 26 April 1963, FO 371/168725/XC7611, PRO.

53. J. B. Kelly, Arabia, *The Gulf and The West,* New York: Basic Books, 1980, p. 143.

54. Kelly, p. 26

55. Glen Balfour-Paul, *The End of Empire in the Middle East,* London: Cambridge, 1991, p. 149.

56. Kelly, pp. 49-50.

Sultan Qaboos bin Said Al-Said

6

SULTAN QABOOS

The coup that sent Sultan Said into exile paved the way for development in the sultanate. Sultan Qaboos bin Said was committed to using the resources available to build a modern state. He wished to end the isolation of his country, to join the Arab world and the international community. The task was formidable, the obstacles numerous. He was challenged by rebels and foreign powers. He was hampered by some subjects who resisted change and others who demanded immediate transformation. He was fortified simultaneously by his heritage -- his legitimacy as a member of the Al Bu Said family -- by continued British support, and gradually increasing American support.

After Sultan Qaboos deposed his father on July 23, 1970, he traveled to Muscat. Omanis were delighted to receive their new ruler. The population of the capital area was so happy that the people carpeted the entire area of Muscat and Mutrah with rugs.[1] Following his arrival from Salalah, the new sultan addressed the nation:

> We hope that this day will mark the beginning of a new age and a great future for us all. We promise you that we shall do our duty towards the people of our dear country. We also hope that every one of you will do his duty in helping us to build the thriving and happy future that we seek for this country, because, as you know,

> unless there is co-operation between the
> government and the people we will not be able
> to build our country with the speed required to
> free her from backwardness she has endured for
> so long. [2]

Qaboos asked all Omanis living outside the country to return to share in the task of constructing a modern state. Tens of thousands who had left Oman in the 1950s and 1960s returned with the skills they had acquired abroad. Most exiles had found opportunity in the Arab world, in the other gulf states, in Egypt, or Iraq. Others had studied in the Soviet Union, motivated less by ideology than by opportunity, and a small number had been educated in the West.

Among the exiles who rejoiced at the sultan's assumption of power was Salim Al Ghazali. Born in Sur in 1948, one of nine children, Ghazali had been taken abroad by his father. Thus, he had the opportunity to go to school in East Africa and later in Egypt. While studying in Cairo for a brief period, Ghazali was affiliated with George Habash's Arab National Movement. He left in 1965 to form a small Omani national organization. Seeking the skills that at that time appeared necessary to accomplish the liberation of Oman, Ghazali and four other members of his group asked the Castro government to admit them to Cuba for guerrilla training. Their request was denied; Ghazali's group applied to the government of Mao Tse-tsung. China accepted the young Omanis. After completing his training in China, Ghazali attempted to enter Oman via Saudi Arabia. The Saudis arrested him. Four months later he escaped and managed to reach Kuwait, where his father served as ambassador of the exiled government of the imamate. Although there was a wide gap between the political views of father and son, both opposed the stagnant regime of Sultan Said bin Taimour.

At this juncture, the Chinese trained fighter went to Algeria to complete formal military studies. After graduation in 1968, Ghazali, who was blacklisted in Oman, had no place to go. He joined the Iraqi army, where he worked training his fellow exiles to topple the Omani regime. When Sultan Qaboos assumed power and called on all exiles to return, like numerous others scattered throughout the world, Ghazali and his entire family responded, discarding a variety of ideologies to pledge loyalty to the sultan and aid in the creation of a modern state.

Sayyid Tariq, who had never before met his nephew the sultan, returned from exile to serve as prime minister. Prior to the coup, the government had only two ministries, interior and foreign affairs. Like, his father Qaboos kept direct control of defense, finance, petroleum affairs, Dhofar, and the Muscat area. Tariq quickly formed new ministries, education, health, justice, information, labor, social affairs, and economy. Here was a cabinet of national reconciliation with few ties to the old order. Foreigners were excluded from the cabinet. Although a majority of ministerial posts were controlled by members of the royal family, many, like Tariq, had gone into exile rather than live under the tyranny of the old regime.[3]

There is evidence that uncle and nephew, the sultan and his prime minister, developed a relationship of mutual respect. At the same time, there were problems of communication and differences of opinion. Shortly after assuming the position of prime minister, Tariq departed for Europe, both to settle personal affairs and to win diplomatic recognition for the sultanate. His absence reduced the opportunity for the two to develop a working relationship. Gossip circulated within both the sultan's and the prime minister's circles. Sometimes it appeared that Qaboos and Tariq were working on opposite sides, that Tariq wanted a quick transition to a western style constitutional monarchy and the new sultan wished to retain the traditional powers of his office. Tensions increased. As a result Tariq resigned in December 1971.

In June 1994, discussing the association between his father and his cousin, the sultan, Undersecretary of State for Foreign Affairs Sayyid Haitham said:

> My father was too liberal at the wrong time. As prime minister Tariq wanted to move too fast at a time when Oman knew nothing of what he was talking about. His Majesty thought that it was necessary to move much slower, but there has never been any bitterness. The sultan and Tariq were close. His Majesty never really replaced my father with anybody else. He took on the responsibility himself.[4]

After resigning as prime minister, Tariq remained an active adviser to the sultan. He headed the Omani delegation to talks with Iran on the median line in the Strait of Hormuz, accompanied the sultan on numerous missions, including the Arab Summit Conference in Algiers in November 1973, to Iran in March 1974, and to the United States in January 1975.[5] Tariq died in 1981 in a London hospital. His body was immediately flown home. Thousands of mourners stood in the streets of Muscat. The sultan, members of the royal family, and government ministers walked behind his coffin, which was draped in the Omani colors; red, white, and green. Mourning was observed for forty days; no palace receptions were held; racing at Seeb and New Year's Eve programs scheduled by Muscat's hotels were canceled. Referring to Tariq, one caption in the government owned *Times of Oman* read, "Always there to help His Majesty."[6]

Sayyid Tariq had lived long enough to witness dramatic changes in the sultanate. Muscatis were no longer burdened by the onerous regulations such as those that had ordered the city's gates closed at sunset, and forbade the repair of homes without permission. A year after the arrival of Sultan Qaboos in Muscat, Omanis enjoyed the end of the ban on smoking in the streets. Ironically, twenty four years later many ministries banned smoking on their premises, and the ministry of health attempted to end smoking, not by decree, but through a media education campaign.[7] During the first year after liberation from the tyranny of Sultan Said, the new government continued to lift restrictions. The gate of the old town no longer closed at nine o'clock and groups of men remained outside the gate, gossiping as long as they pleased.[8] Members of the business elite and the educated Omanis formed clubs. One such club was the Nasser, where the young sultan's portrait shared wall space with a picture of the late Egyptian ruler.[9]

Sultan Qaboos was determined to rule a unified country. No longer would the sultanate be known as Muscat, Oman and Dependencies. Speaking on the radio in August 1970 the sultan announced that, henceforth, the name of his country was the Sultanate of Oman. The sultan's most pressing of the myriad of problems was, of course, the task of ending the rebellion in Dhofar, an insurrection that had become a focal point for all radical political movements in the Arabian peninsula. Supported by China and supplied by the People's Democratic Republic of Yemen, the rebels had two goals: to topple traditional rulers and force Britain to leave the gulf. With the rebellion a major concern, Sultan Qaboos visited the White House in January 1975. A memorandum from Secretary of State Henry Kissinger to President Gerald R. Ford stated:

> Maintaining Oman's stability in the face of this war is a great concern to both the Saudis and Iranians. The Shah, King Faisal and other moderate Arab leaders are encouraging us to

develop closer relations with Oman, particularly since its strategic location at the mouth of the Gulf means that two-thirds of the world's oil exports transit its territorial waters.[10]

Anticipating reporters questions following the sultan's meeting with the president, the State Department prepared a draft statement for the possible use of the White House press secretary. The statement said that Washington welcomed and strongly supported the efforts of all regional states, including Oman, to strengthen security. The only American program in the sultanate at that time was a thirty-member Peace Corps operation. The White House planned to declare that no new programs were discussed. Nevertheless, the United States would "be as responsive as possible" to any Omani request for aid.[11] A *Washington Post* article reported that the sultan was not offered American weapons, but that when the sultan hosted a reception at Blair House "some pretty big guns attended," including Secretary of Defense James Schlesinger and William Colby, director of the Central Intelligence Agency.[12] After the sultan's visit to the United States, cooperation between Washington and Muscat increased.

The northern portion of Oman, engrossed in the creation of government and business, ignored the war; the south did not have that luxury. With encouragement from the United States and increased aid from Britain, the SAF began an aggressive campaign against the rebels. At the same time, unlike his father, Sultan Qaboos was sincerely committed to reconciliation. He announced a pardon for all rebels who surrendered and honored his promise. As a result, dissatisfied tribesmen defected and joined the forces loyal to the sultan. The wali of Dhofar, Buraik bin Hamud al Ghafiri, headed the new Dhofar Development Committee and coordinated intelligence and military activity. The government established a Dhofar Brigade with 10,000 men. This was a multinational force, consisting of Omani -- mostly Baluchis -- British, Iranians, and Jordanians. The rebels responded to the challenge with the party conference in June 1971 that adopted the name Popular Front for the Liberation of Oman and the Arab Gulf (PFLOAG).

The cost of fighting the rebels was substantial; the war diverted revenue from development programs and posed a constant threat to the internal security of the country. However, disagreement among the rebels increased -- between committed Marxists and Dhofari nationalists. The government gained an important victory in April 1972, when during Operation Simba the Dhofar Brigade occupied Sarfait near the South Yemen border. The PFLOAG responded with an offensive that failed. At this juncture, the Chinese withdrew support. Nevertheless, the war continued. The rebels held yet another conference in May 1974 and renamed themselves the Popular Front for the Liberation of Oman (PFLO). At the beginning of December 1975, for the first time since Operation Simba, ground troops, rather than air force, reached the Sarfait battalion. The sultan was notified that Dhofar was secure for civil development. Although Sultan Qaboos announced the end of the war on 11 December, terrorist activity continued. Soviet, East German, and Cuban advisers remained in the People's Democratic Republic of Yemen. A normalization agreement between Oman and South Yemen was not reached until November 1982.[13]

Arab nations assisted in the task of ending the threat to the sultanate. Jordan and Saudi Arabia contributed substantial aid. Iran, too, made an important contribution. Intent on establishing Iran as the regional superpower, the shah supplied 3,000 men to the effort to defeat the rebels in Dhofar.[14] Visiting England in April 1973, Iranian Premier Amir Abbas Hoveyda told reporters that the government of Oman had asked for Iranian assistance. Hoveyda said that Teheran would help the sultan because Iran could not allow its economic lifeline -- the Persian Gulf and the Strait of Hormuz -- to be in the hands of "subversive elements."[15] The British military also participated. Her Majesty's Royal Army Engineers remained in Oman and assisted in the development of the Dhofar region. They built roads on the Jebel, sometimes under fire and always at the risk of encountering enemy mines. British squadrons worked throughout Dhofar, carrying out both military and civilian operations. They built community centers, clinics, shops, schools, and even Mosques. The engineers, who did not leave Oman until December 1977, were publicly thanked by the Muscat government for helping to end terrorism by constructing the Hornbeam Line -- a barrier leading northwards from above Mughsay that denied terrorists access to East Dhofar. These Britons were also praised for training the sultan's engineers and other sections of the Omani army.[16]

The rebellion was crushed but, South Yemen with its strong ties to communist states remained a source of concern, the enemy within the Arab gates. Official Oman declared that friendship with Russia was like, "keeping snakes as pets." In vain the sultan expressed the wish that South Yemen would stop interfering in the internal affairs of the sultanate.[17] In Muscat for a brief period, it appeared that Saudi financial aid might move

Aden to abandon its close relationship with Moscow and that the South Yemeni leaders might return to the "beliefs of their fathers." Alas, by the end of December 1977 it was obvious that the People's Republic on the Omani border accepted gifts, but rejected advice. Then after the assassination of North Yemen's President, Ahmed Hussein Al-Ghashmi, in the summer of 1978, a murder for which Aden was considered responsible, the Arab League Council imposed sanctions that called for a freeze on diplomatic and political relations with South Yemen. The league also called for the suspension of economic and technical aid. Muscat considered the sanctions to be "just retribution."[18]

Tribal contingents paid tribute to the sultan in Salalah during September 1978. An editorial in the *Times of Oman* mused that only a few years before fighting took place in Dhofar, perhaps some of the tribesmen now saluting the sultan had earlier been rebels. The happy result was a credit to Sultan Qaboos, who understood that the rebels were not truly Marxists but had been motivated to rebel because living conditions were unbearable. Now the once isolated and backward Jebel was the location of modern villages, linked by good roads. The former rebels had returned to allegiance to His Majesty "without dishonour."[19] In addition to insuring the nation's tranquillity through economic development, the sultanate developed a powerful military force. The mission of the military was to defend the country against foreign aggression, but at the same time, the military was prepared to maintain domestic security. The cost was high. Expenditures on defense and security in Oman in 1989 equaled 43.2 percent of the total budget.[20]

Immediately after the coup, the enormous problems involved in establishing adequate health care, education, and communications were addressed. The first minister of health, Dr. Asim Al Jamali, who had trained in Karachi, inherited few medical services. Malaria, trachoma and tuberculosis were common. The infant mortality rate was 75 to 80 percent. Many children died of malaria by age five. To meet the pressing need for health care, the government began the construction of regional hospitals. Meanwhile, the World Health Organization offered assistance. The number of practicing doctors in the sultanate rose from ten, at the time of the coup, to forty a year later.[21] As a subsequent minister of health, Dr. Ali Moosa declared:

> Things that happened in this country in one generation took in the west hundreds of years. We were lucky. Change came at the right time

so we had the political will to accept that
change. People were eager and ready. We had
the right leadership. [22]

Equally important, the price of oil increased and the sultanate
had the financial ability to benefit from all the available
technology. [23]
    One physician who responded to the sultan's call to assist
in the development of the country was Dr. Wahid Al Khaursi.
Born in Zanzibar and educated in England, together with many
Omanis of Zanzibari descent, Khaursi, came to Oman. When he
arrived in Muscat in 1971, the country's only hospital was the
missionary hospital in Mutrah, which was then under the
administration of the ministry of health. There were several
other individual doctors who ran clinics in other parts of the
country, and some doctors with the army. Most were Indians.
When the ministry of health was established, the men in charge
knew little about the country. They first had to explore in order
to plan medical services.
    One of the initial tasks of the Ministry of Health was to
develop vaccination programs and a department of maternal and
child health in order to reach a standard of infant mortality that
was within internationally acceptable levels. An increase in
piped water together with an educational program that explained
the necessity of boiling water led to a decrease in dysentery.
Malaria, however, remained difficult to control. Swamps were
drained and spraying after every rain fall was begun. Soon
schools, radio, and television were available to educate the
public about cleanliness. Twenty four years later, Omani
physicians were able to give equal attention to prevention and
cures. Speaking in May 1994, two months prior to the
graduation of the Oman medical school's first class of forty five
doctors, Dr. Khaursi said:

> We hope that our doctors will not all want to be
> surgeons, that they'll go into things like school
> health, community and family medicine. We
> have managed to curtail all the diseases of
> nature, colds, and coughs. We are seeing more
> cancer than ever before. Is it that people are
> seeing physicians, or that we have improved our
> diagnostic facilities? Before we didn't have
> records! In the early 70's it was rare to do an
> appendectomy -- now an appendectomy is a
> common thing. Is it diet? Or pollution, even

> though we are almost pollution free? His
> Majesty is very keen on environmental control.
> Is it the problems of heat and sun?[24]

In 1994, Oman's population grew at an annual rate of
4.86 percent -- faster than that of any other country.[25] Although
birth control is a controversial issue in Islam, the sultan,
advocated birth spacing. As a result, all birth control methods
were available in 1994. Abortion, however, remained illegal
unless the mother's life was in danger and the risk was certified
by more than one doctor.

Despite the rapid changes in Oman, considerable
emphasis on tradition remained. Most Omani men wore
traditional dress, dishdashas (long robes), sandals, and turbans.
The Ministry of Health mandated that all male doctors, except
pediatricians who might frighten children with their strange
western outfits, dress in short-sleeved shirts, ties, trousers and
shoes. Initially, the dress code was established because

> most of the doctors at the time were expatriates.
> Imagine telling an English doctor or an Indian
> doctor you must wear a dishdasha to come to
> work! We are a very tolerant society. All the
> instruction from above is that we have to respect
> our expatriate colleagues in all the fields here.[26]

Oman's first medical students trained in the sultanate, in what
was both an assertion of self-confidence and an expression of
national pride, requested that they be permitted to wear national
dress.[27]

Together with health care, the establishment of an
education system received priority. When Sultan Qaboos
assumed power throughout the sultanate only 900 boys attended
school, other than classes in Koranic studies. In the Koranic
schools, boys learned the Koran by heart. In the absence of
paper, the shoulder blades of camels served as notebooks. No
girls attended school. By May 1977, 64,975 boys and girls were
enrolled.[28] The Ministry of Education was not only concerned
with educational opportunities for school age children of both
sexes, but also with providing an opportunity for older Omanis
who never before had the chance to learn to read and write. In
order to wipe out illiteracy, the ministry opened centers
throughout the country. In September 1980, Minister of
Education, Yahya bin Mafhudh Al Mantheri thanked the United
Nations Educational, Scientific, and Cultural Organization for

assistance in establishing these centers.[29]   The number of
students -- more than half girls -- taking the examination to
receive the General Secondary School Certificate in 1994
reached 14,000. The examination was held in 154 centers
located in every section of the sultanate.[30]

After the establishment of the Ministry of Education,
teachers were hired from abroad. Initially the majority came
from Arab countries. To facilitate the Omanization of the
teaching profession, the first teacher-training institute in the
sultanate opened in 1976. Then in 1982 the foundation stone for
Sultan Qaboos University was laid. Classes began four years
later, with English as the language of instruction in many fields.
Again, of course, the majority of the faculty came from abroad.
The sultan's objective was to establish a world-class university.
Achieving this goal necessitated hiring the best possible faculty.
Here was a difficult problem. According to journalist Liesl Graz,
although there was a large pool of available Egyptian academics
for hire, Muscat was reluctant to rely on Egyptians, who were
often disliked "for their rapacity and mediocrity."[31] It was easier
to blame outsiders, but the core of the problem was that the
Omani desire to preserve tradition sometimes conflicted with
academic freedom. Scholarship was censored and visiting
academics wishing to keep their positions acquiesced

Free education through the university level was
guaranteed to all Omanis, men and women. Students from other
member states of the Gulf Cooperation Council (GCC), Bahrain,
Kuwait, Qatar, Saudi Arabia, and the United Arab Emirates, may
also attend the university without paying tuition. During the
1988-1989 academic year approximately 25 percent of the total
population of Oman was enrolled in school. Forty-five percent
of those enrolled were female.[32] Omanis were not satisfied with
only increasing the pool of students attending school. They
remained concerned about improving the quality of the education
available. An editorial in the *Times of Oman* asked, "Is all well
with Arab education?"   The author complained that the
educational system prevailing in the Arab world stressed
memorization and neglected critical thinking. He suggested that
rather than focus on trivial matters and on the large number of
graduates, Arab educators should improve their methodology.[33]

Education has been an important factor in changing the
status of women. For example, traditionally only men shopped
and some conservative Omanis continue to limit the activities of
women; however, a large number of Omani women strolled
through Muscat's modern shopping centers in 1994. "My own
mother goes to the Souk," reported Sayyid Haitham.[34] Education

also reduced the likelihood that a man would take more than one wife. The custom continued, but as education increased the number of men who exercised the option declined. Educated women began to express their own opinions. At the same time, economic progress provided Omanis with the means to acquire an air-conditioned house furnished with all the modern appliances. Given the conditions of contemporary Omani life men, can no longer afford more than one family.[35] However, some conservative Omanis remained uncomfortable with the change in the role of women, and the government moved to allay their fears. For example, the new university was constructed with separate walking paths for men and women.

Prior to the arrival of Sultan Qaboos in Muscat the absence of paved roads -- ten kilometers in the entire sultanate -- effectively separated the various areas of the country. Villages in the interior lived in virtual isolation from one another. The government gave priority to road transport, and in addition to 19,000 kilometers of unsurfaced roads, by 1990 the country had a network of 4,000 kilometers of surfaced roads, which met the highest international standards. Omanis enjoyed their roads, but drove so fast that in March 1976 every third accident resulted in a death or serious injury. After the introduction of speed limits and Oman's first traffic lights, casualties on the road were reduced. However, traffic accidents remained a problem. The *Times of Oman* in December 1977 pointed out that some people only obeyed the rules if policemen were on patrol.[36] Crime was not a problem in Oman, nor was suicide or alcohol abuse. Most trauma cases brought to Khoula hospital in 1994 resulted from traffic accidents.[37] In charge of ports, airports, and roads, Minister of Communication Salim Al Ghazali explained, "Driving fast is a hobby, like watching football." While the Omani police worked hard to educate people, beautiful roads encouraged fast driving.[38]

At the time the sultan began the modernization of the country, he also embarked on a campaign to end the seclusion imposed by his father. Sultan Said, proud of the distinct character of the Ibadhi sect, had not thought of himself as an Arab and had never expressed an inclination to enter the Arab world.[39] Sultan Qaboos, however, wanted Oman to participate in both Arab affairs and in the international community. Oman's efforts to end its isolation succeeded in 1971, when the sultanate was admitted to the Arab League and the United Nations, although without the support of Saudi Arabia. The sultanate and Saudi Arabia had no fixed borders, and the Saudis, who continued to support the imamate, remained angry as a result of the unresolved Buraimi dispute. Desiring to heal the breach, the sultan, whose first official foreign trip had been to Iran, accepted an invitation to visit Riyadh at the end of 1971. After receiving Sultan Qaboos, Saudi Arabia extended full diplomatic relations to the sultanate. Three years later, the Buraimi dispute was finally concluded when Riyadh withdrew the Saudi claim to the nine disputed villages. Abu Dhabi and Oman divided the villages between them.[40] The breach was healed. One indication of the warm relationship that developed between Muscat and Riyadh was an article in the *Times of Oman* at the end of 1977; the article called King Khalid the Arab ruler most often consulted by foreign powers; Saudi Arabia's place in world affairs was a tribute to his leadership, as well as recognition of the status of Saudi Arabia as the world's largest oil producer.[41] Meanwhile, Oman and Iraq established diplomatic relations in 1976. At the same time, the sultan continued to cultivate good relations with Iran. The shah visited Muscat in December 1977 to discuss commercial ties and future economic collaboration. In addition, he reasserted an earlier promise of cooperation to safeguard international navigation in the Strait of Hormuz, which at its narrowest point measures less than twenty-four miles. An editorial in the *Times of Oman* stated that the two countries, Oman and Iran, were not divided by a narrow strait of water, but rather linked by that strait.[42]

At this juncture, the sultanate was concerned with the development of a gulf security policy based on cooperation among the gulf states and linked to American and British guarantees. In November 1976, the sultan, invited all the foreign ministers in the gulf, to a meeting in Muscat. No agreement was reached. Then a Marxist regime took over Afghanistan; Ethiopia moved against Eritrea; Egypt progressed toward peace with Israel. Meanwhile, unrest in Iran increased and finally led to the fall of the shah and the establishment in January 1979 of an Islamic republic under the leadership of Ayatollah Khomeini. The shah had been a firm supporter of the sultan. With his departure, the sultanate became more vulnerable. Although the Omani Navy had only six small patrol boats, Sultan Qaboos became the protector of western interests in the Strait of Hormuz. Washington now decided that in the event of an attack by the Soviets, the United States would defend Oman. Despite Iraqi objection, the sultanate in 1980 agreed to an access agreement with the United States. From 1977 Washington had sought access to the Masirah air base; the agreement provided for American access to that base, as well as to bases at Khasab, Sib, and Thamarit. In addition, Americans were given access to naval bases at Muscat and Salalah. The agreement stipulated that Omani approval must be sought prior to the utilization of these bases and that American troops could not be stationed in the sultanate. The understanding included an American promise of military and economic assistance. Washington paid the cost of improving the bases, including the construction of a new runway at Khasab. The agreement was renewed in 1985, and at this juncture the sultanate gave the United States the right to pre-position military equipment in Oman.[43] In "the old days" British ties were the result of personal relationships -- it was person to person. After Oman became a modern state, however, the system changed. "The Sultanate regards America as a pillar of stability and good relations with Washington are very important."[44]   At the same time, following Omani tradition, throughout his reign Sultan Qaboos and his government have sustained a uniquely Omani policy and steadfastly maintained an independent voice. Omani autonomy was illustrated in 1985 when the sultanate recognized the Soviet Union -- Muscat now had the confidence to handle snakes.

When war between Iran and Iraq began in September 1980, Oman's neighbors were prepared to work together on a joint defense policy. Saudi Arabia invited the foreign ministers to Riyadh in February 1981 to establish what became the Gulf Cooperation Council. (GCC)[45] Oman played an active role in maintaining the organization, in 1989 hosting the heads of state of the Arab Gulf community. Achieving tranquillity in the gulf was no easy task as the area moved from crisis to crisis. After the Iranian Revolution in 1979, relations between Muscat and Tehran had deteriorated, but by 1985 and 1986 relations were normalized. At a Tunis meeting of Arab foreign ministers in September 1987, Oman, once again acted independently, refusing to participate in a declaration condemning the regime of Ayatollah Khomeini.[46] Referring to Iran in 1994, Sayyid Haitham declared: "We have a healthy relationship with Iran, mostly a political relationship. It's a large country. It's our neighbor. Whatever happens in Iran has an effect on our part of the world."[47]

The end of the Iran-Iraq War did not bring peace to the region. Iraq, which twenty nine years before had been prevented by British intervention from invading Kuwait, in August 1990 occupied that country. Muscat had attempted to persuade the Iraqi ruler, Saddam Hussein, not to pursue an aggressive course. Even after the Iraqi invasion of Kuwait, the Omani government tried to convince the Iraqi dictator to relinquish aggression. Neither Omani trade nor Omani communications were affected, but Oman joined the American led United Nations effort to liberate occupied Kuwait. According to Sayyid Haitham Oman participated "because we are a member of the GCC. It was our obligation, our duty."[48]

Among the criteria for acceptance into the brotherhood of Arab states and membership in the Arab League was condemnation of Israel. Although prior to 1970 the government of the sultanate had no interest in the Arab-Israeli conflict. Sultan Qaboos was obligated to champion the Palestinian cause, or at the very least to pay lip service to the war against Israel because he sought a role in Arab affairs. In his speech to the nation on the occasion of Oman's fourth National Day the sultan said:

> Our people participated in the battle of the Arab nation in its struggle against the common Zionist enemy. They did this by the sheer belief in the oneness of the Arab nation to whom we also belong and share its destiny and battles and also in the solution of its problems and causes. This was unequivocally demonstrated in the war of 6th October (10 Ramadan) when our Arab forces humbled the arrogance of the Zionist enemy, and the Arab forces crossed the barriers into Victory. Such participation has since materialized into real common action -- epitomizing Arab unity in its real sense. [49]

Oman benefited from the Arab oil boycott that followed the 1973 Egyptian led attack on Israel, known in the Arab world as the Ramadan War. High oil prices provided a sharp increase in profits to spend on development. But Israel posed no threat to Oman and the Sultanate refused to march in step with Arab states that rejected accommodation with the Jewish state. While maintaining the Arab economic boycott of Israel, the sultan publicly supported a solution that included Arab recognition of Israel in return for Israeli recognition of Palestinian rights and the restoration of East Jerusalem to Arab sovereignty. As a result, Oman stood alone among all the Arab countries and supported Egyptian President Sadat's efforts to achieve peace with Israel. Defending Egypt, the sultan declared that "disputes within the Arab Community should be settled, either by quiet diplomacy, or around the conference table." The Omani government called for harmony: "The initiative which is now needed is one which will seek out, if not common ground for a peace settlement with Israel, at least a basis for peaceful cooperation among the Arab states."[50]   Oman continued to support Egypt.[51] In 1980 the sultan asserted that President Ronald Reagan's resolute support for Israel would not have any impact at all on American-Omani relations. According to Sultan Qaboos, despite all the difficulties involved, the agreement between Egypt and Israel was the appropriate way to resolve the conflict. "Up to now, no one has come up with a better approach."[52]   Following the Israeli expulsion of the Palestine Liberation Organization (PLO) from Beirut, Sultan Qaboos told American journalist Strobe Talbott in October 1982 that the most likely solution for the Palestinians was a Jordanian-Palestinian confederation. The sultan expressed optimism that his own standing in the Arab world would be strengthened as a result of the American role in arranging for the PLO evacuation. Referring to his long- standing advocacy of friendship with the United states and compromise with Israel, the sultan said, "I think many rather envy us for pulling through and for sticking to our position."[53]

Speaking in May 1994, Minister of Information Abdul Aziz Al Rowas said that Omanis don't believe in confrontation. "We didn't boycott Egypt when the rest did. It wasn't easy, but what is easy in life?" Referring to the Declaration of Principles signed by Israel and the PLO, Al Rowas called the peace process an opportunity not to be lost.

> Peace should be given a chance to evolve -- a fair chance.   The two parties, the Labor government in Israel, the PLO, have crossed the fence. I don't see a retreat. Give them a chance! Israel must withdraw from South Lebanon, the sooner the better. Israel should give back the Golan Heights and we shall have a new era.[54]

In April 1994, Oman became the first Arab Gulf state to host an official Israeli delegation when forty four Israelis, led by Deputy Foreign Minister Yossi Bellin, arrived in Muscat to participate in multilateral water talks attended by delegates from thirty seven countries. Oman sought Israeli counsel on water problems and expertise on desalination projects. The shortage of water in the sultanate was a result of many factors. The population had increased to include more than 2 million Omanis and hundreds of thousands of guest workers. Prior to 1970, the amount of water that an entire Omani family used daily, was not enough for even one person twenty four years later. Omanis require water for dishwashers, washing machines, gardens, and swimming pools, and Oman in 1994 did not have the water resources to satisfy the demand.[55]

Both Iran and Syria criticized the sultanate for holding the talks with Israeli participation. Syria's official daily, *Tishreen*, asked, "Is it logical to hold meetings in Arab capitals to discuss cooperation with Israel while, Israel practices the law of the jungle against millions of Arabs and continues to occupy their lands?" Meanwhile, Iran's state radio complained, "It is amazing that countries without diplomatic relations with the Zionist regime are welcoming these occupiers whose hands are drenched with the blood of innocent Palestinians."[56]

The sultan ignored these complaints. Discussing talks with the Israelis, Sayyid Haitham said, "we want to benefit and we want to push the peace process forward. It was very successful. It was a breakthrough in pushing the peace process, and preparing the ground for further such meetings."[57]

Nevertheless, Oman was unwilling to sign a peace treaty with Israel. Minister of State for Foreign Affairs Yusuf bin-Alawi told Israeli journalists that a treaty between Israel and Oman was impossible until Israel achieved a permanent peace with all of its neighboring states. He reminded the Israelis that they had conquered Arab lands. He also remarked that Israel is not located in Europe, but in the Middle East.[58] Nevertheless, progress toward normal relations continued. American companies exporting to Israel had problems gaining access to the Omani market in 1993 and asked the State Department to intercede. Finally Oman and its five partners in the Gulf Cooperation Council in September 1994 ended the blacklisting of American and foreign companies that traded with Israel, thus removing another stumbling block on the road toward resolution of the Arab-Israeli conflict. Members of the GCC pledged to influence other Arab states to follow their example and drop all trade restrictions involving Israel.[59]

Speaking before the United Nations General Assembly at the end of September, Foreign Minister bin Alawi reaffirmed Oman's desire to promote the settlement of all disputes among the nations in the region and to work toward achieving stability in the Arab Gulf. He expressed the sultanate's satisfaction with the progress achieved in resolving the Arab-Israeli conflict.

> The spirit of hatred and enmity between the Arabs and Israel has begun to wane and is being gradually replaced by a climate of mutual understanding, dialogue and concord. We are fully convinced that we and Israel have no

option but to sit down at the negotiating table
and resolve our differences by peaceful means.
Some promising results have already been
achieved, despite the fact that we are still at the
beginning of the road and there is still a long
way to go, and deep differences remain.[60]

Autocratic regimes, of course, prevail in the Middle East
and political participation is limited. The sultan continued to
rule according to Muslim precepts and in keeping with tribal
conditions. After the collapse of the Dhofar rebellion in 1975,
candid political opposition disappeared. Omanis were occupied
with the construction of the state. All government employees
entering the civil service between 1974 and 1987, whatever their
function, were required to take an oath composed by Director of
Intelligence Ray Nightingale. Each new employee swore
allegiance to His Majesty the Sultan.[61] With the sultan's
approval, the oath was amended in 1987 so that new members
were required to swear allegiance not to the ruler, but to *al-watan
al-'Umani* (the Omani nation).[62] In 1981 Sultan Qaboos
appointed a state consultative council, which rarely met and had
little power. Although it appeared that he was under no pressure
to do so, in November 1990 the sultan announced the
establishment of a new consultative council. During the spring
of 1991 the governors of Oman's fifty-nine administrative
provinces assembled the notable men of their provinces. From
each assembly three were chosen as candidates. Their names
were submitted to the sultan, who selected fifty nine men, one
from each province. The end result was a consultative council
mostly of tribal leaders and businessmen. Government officials
were excluded. Addressing the Council in December 1991, the
sultan declared that it was an equal branch of government, not
subject to the executive branch. The council had no power to
question foreign and defense policy but had a mandate to look at
all domestic issues, and even question ministers before television
cameras.[63] Although the electronic media are owned and
operated by the government, the media enjoyed a greater degree
of freedom than similar media in other Middle Eastern
countries.[64] Criticism of the sultan, however, remained
forbidden. Reproaching foreign heads of state was a different
matter. Discussing American President Jimmy Carter in
September 1980, the *Times of Oman* suggested that he had real
courage because in an election year Carter signed legislation for
a program to accelerate widespread use of wind energy. The
newspaper commented that the American president "may well be

blown away in the gales of laughter, which will surely mark such legislative timing."[65]

Most Omanis appeared to be satisfied with their political system, a system that still prohibited political parties and independent labor unions, a system in which the state controlled all radio and television, and at the same time closely supervised all newspapers. In 1994, the sultanate, was not ready for constitutional monarchy. It will be some years until all adults are educated and every shaikh of every tribe is a graduate of some sort. Meanwhile, every Omani has gained from the development that Sultan Qaboos began. As a result of profits from the sale of oil, a considerable variety of services are available to all citizens. Omanis pay no taxes and as is the case with education, receive free health care. In Muscat the streets are cleaned and the gardens watered by an army of Pakistanis and Bangladeshis. A large number of Omani have the means to employ live-in maids from the Philippines. In 1994, Muscatis, had a comfortable lifestyle. On a summer evening it was difficult to find a parking space in the lots of the shopping malls. On behalf of the Ministry of Electricity, the *Oman Daily Observer*, in June 1994, asked all of its dear consumers to switch off one air conditioner to reduce costs and to insure no interruption of electricity.[66]

Personal economic interests are most often related to the state. A majority of Omanis are government employees.[67] Although Oman established a blueprint for privatization of the economy, in 1994 the state sector included the Public Authority for Stores and Food Reserves, the Public Authority for Marketing Agricultural Produce, the Oman Cement Company, the Oman Newspaper House, the Central Bank of Oman, and additional banks for housing, development, agriculture, and fisheries.[68] Oman had 81,000 civil servants in 1994, at least a quarter still expatriates who are excluded from obtaining citizenship. Minister of Civil Service Ahmed Macki explained that there is fat in every government civil service. It is important to trim that fat, but difficult to do so. In 1991, the government, inaugurated a conservative recruitment policy. Not every Omani high school or university graduate was accepted just for the sake of providing employment. "We don't want to convert the government into a social security system." Such a policy would be counterproductive. Only those needed are employed. The demand for Omani engineers, doctors, accountants, veterinarians, lawyers, however, remained greater than the supply. In 1991 the government also inaugurated an Omanization policy to replace foreigner workers with the sultan's subjects. The purpose was not to Omanize simply for the sake of Omanizing, but to do so for the sake of productivity. Carefully selected Omani students were sent abroad at government expense to study a variety of subjects, from English secretarial skills to Arabic accounting. After completing their courses, they returned home to work under the direction of an expatriate in their field before receiving independent status.[69]

Twenty four years after the palace coup that brought Sultan Qaboos to power, the infrastructure of a modern state was complete. But diversifying the economy remained a serious issue. "It's easier to say than to do," lamented Dr. Moosa. Economic development depends on natural resources. Unfortunately, there is insufficient water for the agricultural sector, the climate is uncooperative and the know-now lacking.[70] Sayyid Haitham expressed the hope that oil prices would not deteriorate. In 1994 the economy depended on the government. If the government stopped spending, everything slowed down. For diversification it was essential that the public not wait for the government to spend, that the private sector sponsor programs.[71]

Difficult problems continued to plague the gulf region. Civil war in Yemen in the spring of 1994, caused concern, and the possibility of Islamic extremism remained a potential danger. Meanwhile, in the autumn the Iraqi dictator, Saddam Hussein, who still claimed Kuwait, moved his troops toward the Iraqi-Kuwaiti border. The sultanate used its influence to support accommodation in Yemen, condemnation of extremism, and support for the territorial integrity of Kuwait.

At home Omanis followed their own course, a self-reliant course. Their clothing remained distinctive, their architecture traditional. They insured the protection of wildlife, restored crumbling fortresses, and established history museums. The call to pray continued to be heard, brides still decorated their hands with henna, circumcisions remained occasions for celebration, and the customary coffee pot continued to welcome guests. Sultan Qaboos bin Said achieved his goal; Oman became a participating member of the Arab world and the international community. At the same time, Omanis, proud of their history and zealous to maintain their birthright, remained rooted in their traditions and loyal to their heritage.

NOTES

1. Interview, Hamed Al Rashdi, Muscat, 31 May 1994.

2. Quoted from *The Speeches of H.M. Sultan Qaboos bin Said Sultan of Oman*, 1970-1990, Muscat: Ministry of Information, 1990, p. 11.

3. Calvin Allen, Jr., *Oman: The Modernization of the Sultanate*, Boulder Colo: Westview Press, 1987, p. 81.

4. Interview, Sayyid Haitham, Muscat, 4 June 1994.

5. Ian Skeet, *Oman: Politics and Development*, London: Macmillan, 1992, pp. 58-59.

6. *Times of Oman*, 1 January 1981, p. 1.

7. Interview, Dr. Ali Moosa Muscat, 4 June 1994.

8. Richard Johns, "Muscat: The Way Ahead" in *Middle East International*, Vol. 6, September 1971, p. 7.

9. Ibid., p. 8.

10. Schedule proposal, Kissinger to Ford, Washington, 13 December 1974, Gerald R. Ford Library, Ann Arbor, Michigan (hereafter cited as GRFL).

11. Memorandum, State Department to Scowcroft, Washington, 7 January 1975, GRFL.

12. *Washington Post*, 11 January 1975, p. B3.

13. Allen, Jr., pp. 71-74, and Skeet, pp. 41-52.

14. Peter Mansfield, *A History of the Middle East*, New York: Penguin, 1991, p. 285.

15. Rouhollah Ramazani, *Iran's Foreign Policy*, Charlottesville: University of Virginia, 1975, p. 356.

16. *Times of Oman*, 25 December 1977, p. 15.

17. Ibid., 6 November 1977, p. 1, and *Times of Oman*, 4 December 1977, p. 3.

18. *Times of Oman*, 6 July 1978, p. 1.

19. Ibid., 28 September 1978, p. 3.

20. F. Gregory Gause III, *Oil Monarchies*, New York: Council on Foreign Relations, 1994, pp. 67-68.

21. Richard Johns, "Muscat: the Way Ahead" in *Middle East International*, Vol. 6, September 1971, p. 9.

22. Interview, Dr. ali Moosa, 4 June 1994.

23. Ibid.

24. Interview, Dr. Wahid Al Khaursi, Muscat, 30 May 1994.

25. *New York Times*, 11 September 1994, p. 6.

26. Interview, Dr. Wahid Al Khaursi, Muscat, 30 May 1994.

27. Ibid.

28. *Times of Oman*, 11, December 1977, p. 10.

29. Ibid., 18 September 1980, p. 2.

30. *Oman Daily Observer*, 25 June 1994, p. 1.

31. Liesl Graz, *The Turbulent Gulf*, London: Tauris, 1990, p. 220.

32. Skeet, p. 20.

33. Khaled Al Maeena, "Is All Well with Arab Education?" in the *Times of Oman*, 29 June 1994, p. 6.

34. Interview, Sayyid Haitham, Muscat, 4 June 1994.

35. Interview, Dr. Ali Moosa, 4 June 1994.

36. *Times of Oman*, 25 December 1977, pp. 12 and 14.

37. Interview, Dr. Wahid Al Khaursi, Muscat, May 1994.

38. Interview, Salim Al Ghazali, Mucat, 1 June 1994.

39. Minute, Burrows, London, 10 Setember 1958, FO 371/132626/187320, Public Records Office.

40. Allen, Jr., p. 114.

41. *Times of Oman*, 18 December 1977, p. 3.

42. Ibid., 11 December 1977, p. 3.

43. Allen, Jr., p. 118; and Graz, pp. 225-226.

44. Interview, Sayyid Haitham, Muscat, 4 June 1994.

45. Skeet, pp. 93-94.

46. Graz, p. 226.

47. Interview, Sayyid Haitham, Muscat, 4 June 1994.

48. Ibid.

49. Quoted from *The Speeches of H.M. Sultan Qaboos bin Said Sultan of Oman*, 1970-1990, p. 32.

50. *Times of Oman*, 11 December 1977, p. 3.

51. Skeet, p. 93.

52. Quoted in *Newsweek*, 1 December 1980, p. 46.

53. *Time*, 15 October 1982, p. 50.

54. Interview, Abdul Aziz Al Rowas, Muscat, 29 May 1994.

55. Interview, Dr. Ali Moosa, Muscat, 4 June 1994.

56. *Jerusalem Report*, 26 April 1994, pp. 1-2.

57. Interview, Sayyid Haitham, Muscat, 4 June 1994.

58. *Jerusalem Report*, 26 April 1994, p. 2.

59. *New York Times*, 1 October 1994, p. 1.

60. Text of United Nations Speech by Minister of Foreign Affairs, New York, 29 September 1994.

61. Dale Eickelman and M.G. Dennison, "Arabizing the Omani Intelligence Services: Clash of Cultures?" in *International Journal of Intelligence and Counterintelligence*, Spring 1994, pp. 18-19.

62. Ibid., p. 25.

63. Gause III, pp. 113-114. In 1994 women were elected to the council.

64. Yahya Kamalipour and Hamid Mowlana, *Mass Media in the Middle East*, Westport: Greenwood, 1994, p. 194.

65. *Times of Oman*, 11 September 1980, p. 10.

66. *Oman Daily Observer*, 7 June 1994, p. 1.

67. Gause III, pp. 58-59.
68. Ibid., p. 53.
69. Interview, Ahmed Macki, Muscat, 1 June 1994.
70. Interview, Dr. Ali Moose, Muscat, 4 June 1994.
71. Interview, Sayyid Haitham, Muscat, 4 June 1994.

BIBLIOGRAPHIC ESSAY

British archives are the most important source of available documents in English. For material relating to the period prior to 1945, it is essential to consult the India Office Library in London, and for records pertaining to the post-World War II period, the Public Records Office in Kew. Material relating to the sultanate's American connection is available in the National Archives in Washington DC. In addition, there is a limited amount of accessible material in presidential libraries, including the Roosevelt and Ford Libraries. Although Muscat is reported to have significant papers, the material as yet remains closed to researchers.

Memoirs of westerners who were employed in Oman -- missionaries, government officials, and soldiers -- are another source of interesting material. Missionaries Samuel Zwemer and James Catine recorded their efforts to save souls in *The Golden Milestone,* (New York: Revell, 1940). Government officials including, Thomas Bertram, *Alarms and Excursions in Arabia,* (London: Allen & Unwin, 1931), Sir Ronald Wingate, *Not in the Limelight,* (London: Hutchinson, 1959), and Neil McLeod Innes, *Minister in Oman,* (Cambridge: Oleander, 1987), recorded their efforts both to serve the sultan and at the same time protect British interests. Soldiers David Smiley in *Arabian Assignment*, (London: Cooper, 1975), and P.S. Allfree in *Warlords of Oman*, (London: Hale, 1967), documented their military service in Oman. Journalists too provided impressions of the sultanate, James Morris in *Sultan in Oman,* (London: Farber & Farber,

1957), and Liesl Graz in *The Omanis, Sentinels of the Gulf*, (London: Longman, 1982).

Among the most useful secondary sources for information on the period before World War II are Briton Busch, *Britain and the Persian Gulf, 1894-1914,* (Berkeley: University of California, 1967), Robert Landen, *Oman Since 1856,* (Princeton: Princeton University, 1967), and Sir Harold Wilson, *The Persian Gulf,* (London: Allen & Unwin), 1959.

For the post-World War II period the best secondary sources are J.E. Peterson, *Oman in the Twentieth Century*, (London: Croom Helm, 1986), Ian Skeet, *Muscat and Oman, the End of an Era,* (London: Farber & Farber, 1974), and John Townsend, *Oman, the Making of the Modern State,* (London: Croom Helm, 1977). In addition, F. Gregory Gause III in *Oil Monarchies,* (New York: Council On Foreign Relations, 1994), provides a view of Oman in relation to neighboring Gulf states.

INDEX

About the Author

MIRIAM JOYCE is an Assistant Professor of History at Purdue University, Calumet. She is the author of numerous articles on the Middle East.